Setting Love in Order

There is an enormous amount of unscientific propaganda in circulation denying the reality of sexual redemption in Christ. Here is a book so profound and so vivid as to be undeniable in the truth and promise it presents.

—John H. Rodgers Jr.
Professor, Systematic Theology
Trinity Episcopal School of Ministry
Co-Rector, St. Stephen's Church, Sewickley, Pennsylvania

Of all the passions, perhaps none has so strong a grip on the human soul and psyche as does sexuality. But no compulsion is so powerful that it cannot be broken by genuine faith and healed. As Mario Bergner demonstrates in his gripping autobiography, the modern presumption that sexuality, especially homosexuality, is unchangeable, is a destructive lie.

—Jeffrey Burke Satinover, M.D.
Author of *Homosexuality and the Politics of Truth*

Mario Bergner's story reveals the power of the cross. But instead of causing us to merely rejoice in one man's victory, the truths that Mario discovered over the course of his healing fan out like flames and inspire us on to a deeper and more authentic reliance upon Christ.

—Andy Comiskey
Director of Desert Streams Ministries

Setting Love in Order

Hope and Healing for the Homosexual

Mario Bergner
foreword by Leanne Payne

A Hamewith Book

BakerBooks
A Division of Baker Book House Co
Grand Rapids, Michigan 49516

Published by Hamewith Books
an imprint of Baker Book House Company
P.O. Box 6287, Grand Rapids, MI 49516-6287

Eighth printing, December 2003

Printed in the United States of America

For information about academic books, resources for Christian leaders, and all new releases available from Baker Book House, visit our web site:
http://www.bakerbooks.com/

Library of Congress Cataloging-in-Publication Data

Bergner, Mario, 1958–
    Setting love in order : hope and healing for the homosexual / Mario Bergner.
       p. cm.
    Includes bibliographical references.
    ISBN 0-8010-5186-X
    1. Homosexuality—Religious aspects—Christianity. 2. Church work with gays. 3. Bergner, Mario. 4. Christian biography—United States. 5. Spiritual healing. 6. Men—Psychology. 7. Gay men—Psychology. 8. Prayer—Christianity. I. Title.
    BR115.H6B47   1995
    241'.66—dc20   94-40047

To Annelyse DeBellis and Leanne Payne,
two women whose love for Jesus
and love for me have made me a better man

"As the Father has loved me, so have I loved you; abide in my love."

John 15:9 (RSV)

"Give all for all, look for nothing, ask for nothing in return; rest purely and trustingly in Me, and you shall possess Me. Then you will be free in heart, and no darkness will oppress your soul. Strive for this, pray for this, desire this one thing—that you may be stripped clean of all selfishness, and follow Jesus in complete self-abandonment, dying to self that you may live to Me forever. Then will all vain fantasies be put to flight, and all evil disorders and groundless fears vanish. Then will all fear and dread depart, and all disordered love die in you."

Thomas à Kempis, *The Imitation of Christ*

"The death that he sustained that I might live, and that which every believer hopes, as I do, has drawn me from the sea of perverse love and placed me on the shore of right love.

Dante, *The Divine Comedy*

"Set love in order, thou that lovest me."

Prayer attributed to St. Francis

Contents

Foreword   9
Acknowledgments   11

1 "Choose!"   13
2 Coming Out of Denial: *Facing Evil and Rejection*   33
3 Disordered Love: *The Development of Homosexuality*   55
4 Setting Love in Order: *Disengaging Symbolic Confusion*   73
5 Christ in Us: *The Hope of Glory*   95
6 Loving the Same Sex   113
7 The Hatred of Woman   135
8 Loving the Other Sex   157

Notes   203

Foreword

Setting Love in Order is an important book for many reasons. First of all, many who need deliverance and healing from sexual neuroses will find it even as they read the book. A very sure road to healing is shown to all who desire to travel on it.

There is not a book that better describes (and from the standpoint of one who has suffered intense confusion) what it means to come out of denial about what in fact one's *real problems* are—nor about how one's defenses against evil and deprivation contribute to broken sexuality and development as a homosexual. Mario Bergner describes his sexual neurosis as the "same sex" ambivalence and homosexuality that it was: what that looked and felt like from the inside, and how he came out of it. He also describes his homosexuality as the symbolic confusion that it was, and how he went about disengaging the diseased symbols and replacing them with the healthy ones that the LORD gave him. His sections on misogyny (the hatred of woman) are extraordinary, and he describes as no one else does what "other-sex" ambivalence looks like, and the struggle it takes to free oneself, as a male, from transferences onto woman.

Mario's honesty, with God, himself, and others, is in itself healing. I have never known anyone to self-disclose in the way that he does. In doing so, those who have like needs hear their story. Many realize for the first time, "I'm not the only one who has those feelings," or those "fantasies," or those "fears of falling through the cracks of non-being." Many a soul will, after reading this book, understand for the first time what "separation anxiety" really is, and that there is a healing balm even for this deepest of hurts. In the sharing of all this, the joy of the Lord comes through.

Mario has long had to face human evil, what it is, how it came to be. Once he recognized and named the evil that had so wounded him, he did not shrink back from recognizing it within himself. He named it as he saw it. Why, we may ask, do some people receive so much healing, others so little? To watch Mario or to read his story is to know why. It is because the moment he is aware of sin in his life, he confesses it and turns from it with all his might. He loves the Holy, the beautiful, the just, the true, and knows them to be part of the most exciting quest and journey we can know: that of setting love in order.

Leanne Payne
Pastoral Care Ministries

Acknowledgments

To the Pastoral Care Ministries team, my Christian family—Leanne Payne, Rev. William Beasley and Rev. Anne Beasley, Ariane de Chambrier, Rev. Conlee and Signa Bodishbaugh, Rev. Bob and Connie Boerner, Patsy Casey, Denis Ducatel, John Fawcett, Jean Holt, Jonathan Limpert, Val McIntyre, Dr. Jeffrey Satinover, Ted and Lucy Smith. Together we have traveled the world glorifying God, marveling at His healing power, and storing up happy memories for Heaven.

To friends and fellow laborers in the ministry of sexual redemption—Exodus International in San Rafael, California; Rev. Andy Comiskey and team at Desert Streams, Los Angeles; Rev. Michael Lumberger and team at Dunamis Ministries, Pittsburgh; and Katherine Allen and team at Sought Out Ministries, Virginia Beach—for a unity in Christ that proclaims Jesus forgives and heals homosexuality.

To the faculty, students, and staff at Trinity Episcopal School for Ministry in Ambridge, Pennsylvania, for their prayers, challenges, support, and flexibility with my traveling schedule. To Dr. Stephen M. Smith, my advisor during my seminary years, for his encouragement, and Patricia Miller for graciously tutoring me on the writing and rewriting of this book.

To Hal B. Schell, Rev. David Brown, and my former neighborhood group in Milwaukee for loving and encouraging me early in my healing process.

To special friends around the globe—Rev. Jim and Donna Adkins, Rev. Norman and Jackie Arnold, Rev. David and Jo Blackledge, Ron and Lin Button, Dr. Stuart and Marilyn Checkley, Cliff and Lyn Davis, Kathleen Demien, Rev. Larry and Claudia Evans, Jenny Flanagan, Rev. Joseph Garlington, John and Susan LeCornu, Artemis Limpert, Christiane Mack, Rev. Clay and Mary McLean, Mary Pomrening, Rev. Gerry Soviar, Dr. Daniel Trobisch, and Dr. Roland and Elke Werner—for enriching my life with their prayers, love, and friendship.

To those in the publishing field who have always believed in this book—Lila Bishop, my editor, for her friendship and personal time, Steve Griffith our agent for the Hamewith imprint at Baker Books, and Jan Dennis for encouraging me that this book would appear in print.

To all the above,

> "The Lord bless you and keep you;
> the Lord make his face shine upon you
> and be gracious to you;
> the Lord turn his face toward you
> and give you peace."
>
> Numbers 6:24–26

1

"Choose!"

The LORD will sustain him on his sickbed and restore him from his bed of illness. I said, "O LORD, have mercy on me; heal me, for I have sinned against you."

Psalm 41:3, 4

As I stood in the hospital radiology room getting ready for a chest X-ray, the nurse spoke to me. "Please remove the metal you're wearing around your neck."

Actually it was a uniquely shaped cross with the face of Jesus etched onto it. She must have seen the fear in my eyes as I gently rubbed this precious gift my parents had given me years ago.

"If we wrap it in masking tape, you can keep it on during the X-ray," she said.

"Thank you," I replied.

That symbol of Jesus around my neck was the last vestige of the Christian faith to which I had once looked as a source of hope.

Later in my room, I lay on the hospital bed, feeling empty and afraid as I recounted the events of the last few years. My health over the previous thirteen months had drastically declined. From the first venereal disease in January 1982 to my admission now (February 1983) to Boston City Hospital with thrush, I had had twelve frightening symptoms. In my mind these events occurring within two years after I had become sexually active in New York City pointed in one direction—AIDS.

Five days of blood tests, all of which had returned negative, left only one option—a bone marrow biopsy. This was the only test left to find out why my T-cell count was so low. My doctor had suggested the test earlier, but I had refused to have it done as I knew it was the final test used in diagnosing AIDS. I also feared the pain involved in having this test. However, with no other choice before me and in complete despair, I agreed to undergo the test the next day.

That evening while lying on my bed, I once again gently rubbed the cross that hung around my neck. The name formed on my lips. "Jesus . . . oh, Jesus," I prayed, "what have I done? I sought You out at age fourteen and again at eighteen, but neither time did I receive the healing I needed to be free of homosexuality. Why, Lord? Why are some people able to come to You and enter into the life of the church while others like myself, so clearly in need, fail to get any help at all?"

No answer came. But a vision did. Startled by what I saw, I sat up in my hospital bed. At first I thought, *You're getting hysterical, Mario. Close your eyes and it'll go away.* But even with my eyes closed, I could still see it. I opened my eyes and sat there watching it unfold like a movie playing before me at the foot of my bed.

Two scenes were playing simultaneously on two screens suspended in midair. The screen on the left showed me in a hospital room as a homosexual being treated for AIDS. The screen on the right showed the outline of the Lord's head and shoulders with a great light shining from behind Him. Then the Spirit of the Lord said, "I want to heal your whole person, not just your body. Choose."

Because being healed physically was my only concern at the time, I did not fully understand what healing my "whole person" meant. Still I knew something extraordinarily real was happening, so I chose the screen showing the Lord. As soon as I did, the other screen faded away. Then it seemed as if my whole hospital room was taken up into the screen that remained. I was in the presence of God. I was speechless.

I waited in silence before Him. At first I wondered if this presence were an angel. The light shining from behind was so bright it prevented me from focusing on the face. But now I'm convinced that the presence in my room was, indeed, Jesus. After what seemed a long time, the Spirit of the Lord guided me to pray for myself. He lifted my hands and led me to pray with the laying on of my own hands on my body. I fell asleep with one hand atop of the other resting near my left collarbone.

Once asleep, I dreamed about a girl I had gone to college with in Milwaukee. (Back then I often thought that if I were straight, she would be the kind of girl I would like to marry.) In the dream, we got married. Months later, when Jesus began healing me of the homosexual neurosis, the dream often came to mind. I interpreted it as a promise from God, meaning that one day I would desire a woman and desire to marry her.

Early the next morning, a nurse came in and took one final blood test before the scheduled bone marrow biopsy. A few hours went by. Then my doctor, a young intern, came into my room. Perplexed, he told me that this last blood test had revealed a surprising increase in white blood cells. As a result, he was postponing the biopsy until a new T-cell count could be taken in a few days. I knew then that I had indeed received a healing from Jesus!

After another five days of observation in Boston City Hospital, I was released. My doctor was flabbergasted. I remember the astonished look on his face, his wrinkled forehead, as he shook his head and attributed my miraculous recovery to the nature of the undiagnosed virus that had attacked me.

My doctor ordered me back for a follow-up visit a week later. This time he brought along his supervisor. Together they reviewed my medical records and the alarming immune breakdown that had caused me to be hospitalized. In amazement, this young intern told the older, more experienced doctor that I had already returned to work and that I was exercising at the gym again.

When I chose life during that vision in the hospital, God healed me of my physical illness. Yet I did not fully know I had embarked on a road that eventually would lead me to forsake homosexuality altogether. I had no inkling that my saying yes to Jesus would radically transform every aspect of my life. I only knew I wanted everything He had to give me. My prayer is that all who read this book will say, "Yes, Jesus," and receive His beautiful gifts.

Held in the Hand of God

When I first came to Christ at age fourteen, I was overcome with joy at the thought of eternal life and filled with hope for my future. Though I did not have a name for the confused sexual feelings growing within me, I knew that there was something terribly wrong inside. Unfortunately, the church I attended was not equipped to minister the healing I so desperately needed. They had little understanding of how Christ can redeem a person's sexuality and heal deep emotional wounds.

Nonetheless, God was present in this Bible-believing community. In the year or so that I attended that church, many positive changes occurred in my life. In adopting Christian moral teachings and a Biblical worldview, I began to find a meaningful order to life. Through a powerful teaching series given by the senior pastor on "The Sermon on the Mount," I became a more caring and loving person despite the harsh realities of life at home.

Sometime during that year, for the first time I came across the word *homosexual* in a magazine. I now had a name for the sexual feelings surging uncontrollably within me. As I continued to sit under the preaching of this fine pastor, it became clear that homosexuality was incompatible with Christianity. Because "the homosexual" in me was seemingly growing at a much faster rate than "the Christian" in me, I decided to stop attending church. Still I continued believing in Jesus and living my life according to the Christian standards I had been taught.

For another three years, I struggled silently over my homosexual feelings and Christianity. Deep inside, I feared that if the homosexuality in me was stronger than my Christian faith, then surely Christianity was a religion of unrealistic expectations, empty promises, and false hope. During this time my zeal to live according to Christian standards began to wane.

At age eighteen I heard the remarkable testimony of a former satanic priest turned Christian, and my faith revived. I thought, *Surely if Jesus can set this man free, He can do the same for me.* Yet I chose not to go back into the church because I feared I would find no help there. Secretly, I prayed for more than six months, asking God to direct me to a place where I might find healing for homosexuality. At one point I called the American Psychological Association for the name of a therapist. Because I could not afford therapy nor could I ask my family for the money, I never called for an appointment. My renewed faith soon failed. (I have since discovered that most isolated attempts at Christianity do fail when the new Christian does not find a church home to grow up in.) With no other choice before me, I began accepting my homosexual feelings as a part of myself.

Just before my nineteenth birthday, in the fall of 1977, I entered the University of Wisconsin at Milwaukee (UWM) and majored in theater studies. I met many intelligent and creative homosexual men and women with direction and purpose for their lives. In one way or another they had come to terms with their homosexual orientation. During my first year at UWM, I had a professor who was openly homosexual and who was also very affirming of my acting and singing talents. The more contact I had with these homosexual people, the more I began to feel a kinship with them. I had the same sexual feelings they did, except I kept mine secret and they were open about theirs.

At age twenty-one I moved to New York City after passing the acting audition for admittance to a theater program there. There I came fully "out of the closet" and began openly and freely to acknowledge myself as "gay." For the first time in my life I was telling the truth about my sexual orientation. I experienced a sense of freedom I had never known before. Truth, even about our fallenness, can lift the burden of keeping the masks in place. It wasn't long before I completely identified with my homosexuality. I was gay and began to develop pride in it.

Surprisingly, when I arrived in New York City in the fall of 1980, I found that the same professor from UWM who had been so affirming toward me had also moved to New York City. Both he and his lover had been hired to teach in the theater program where I was enrolled. My friendship with both these men grew, and they became my mentors. They had genuine loving concern for the direction my life was taking and advised me not to invest it in the shallow, narcissistic gay bar scene. Rather, they encouraged me to make something of myself. Oddly enough, I received from them some of the nurturing and affirmation I had always longed for and needed from my father. There was a lot of good in both of these men.

That year I spent Christmas in New York City with friends. On Christmas Eve a group of us, most of whom were gay, decided to go to church. Knowing that a group of homosexual men and women would not be welcome in most churches, I called a gay information hot line to find a church that accepted gays. We were directed to a liturgical worship service for gays sponsored by a mainline denominational church near Union Square.

My friends and I attended the midnight service. The music was beautiful, and the congregation consisted of many gay couples with their arms affectionately around each other. When it came time for the minister to preach, his sermon was about being gay—not about Jesus. He made only passing reference to the birth narrative of Jesus read earlier in the Gospel. The few Biblical passages he referred to were put into the service of his sermon's main theme—on being gay. His preaching did not have the ring of objective truth I had heard in the Biblical preaching of the nondenominational church I had attended as a teenager. Having heard the real thing, I recognized the counterfeit. I left that service more deeply convinced than ever that homosexuality was incompatible with Christianity.

At the end of my first year in New York, my two beloved professor/mentors announced that they would be moving to Boston. The more famous of the two had been hired as a master teacher at a Boston university. When I learned this, I asked him if he would train me to become a teacher of the voice production method in which he was an expert. When he agreed, I dropped out of my school and moved to Boston. Because of the excellent professional reputation of these two men who had trained me, I was hired to teach at the university when they decided to move from Boston a year later.

While I lived in Boston, my involvement in the gay lifestyle increased. Ignoring the advice of my professors, I regularly socialized at gay bars. Sexual activity and drug and alcohol use, which a few years earlier I would never have considered, became part of my life. One bright spot during this time was a friendship between myself and a woman who was also gay. When I was hospitalized in Boston City Hospital, Shauna came to visit me every day and lovingly comforted me. Through her I met many lesbians in the politically active women's community in nearby Cambridge. One of them, a leader in the Massachusetts Gay Political Caucus, jokingly declared my birthday a state holiday.

One autumn evening after having dinner in Harvard Square, Shauna and I went for a walk through the tree-lined streets of Cambridge. In the distance we could see the red brick bell tower of a church. As we approached, we heard a black gospel choir belting out a song about the blood of Jesus. The music was so mesmerizing that we stopped in front of the church and listened. The more the choir sang, the closer we were drawn to the door. Their song was like a gentle wind carefully picking us up as if we were two fallen leaves and drawing us into the back pew of the church.

The singing ended, and a young black preacher gave a sermon on the power of God. While preaching, he strutted up and down the central aisle and even climbed over a few pews. I feared he was making his way toward us. We were the only two white people in the entire church. I envisioned us as two unsightly bleach marks on a beautiful black velvet evening gown. To my relief the preacher did not come near us. Throughout his sermon people shouted "amen" and "that's right!"

When he finished preaching, the congregation broke out into several powerful praise songs. The presence of Jesus filled that little church. Both Shauna and I were speechless. I was near tears. It had been many years since I had felt God's presence.

Still running from the Lord, I chokingly whispered to Shauna, "Let's get out of here before the service ends." Once outside the church, we walked in silence back to Harvard Square, and the sound of singing from the church grew fainter. When we could no longer hear it, Shauna broke the silence. "Mario, this lesbian Jewish girl just felt the presence of Jesus in that church back there." There were tears in her eyes.

In a very weak voice, I replied, "So did I."

We reached Harvard Square and parted company. I took a train home, and Shauna walked to her place. We never mentioned this to one another again.

By October of 1982, the harsh realities of the gay lifestyle were becoming apparent to me. This was my fourth year of living openly as a homosexual. My initial sense of relief at coming out of the closet and enamored fascination with the gay lifestyle had worn away. I had begun to see ugly facets of this way of life—the youth consciousness of the gay community, the sexually trans-mitted diseases I was repeatedly treated for, the devastating breakups with lovers, and the beginnings of the AIDS crisis. These dark clouds of reality loomed over the false promises of happi-ness and freedom held out to young men who are encouraged to embrace homosexuality.

During this time thoughts of my Christian past filled me with pain. It was as if I were a river with two currents set against each other—one which I allowed the world to see, my homosexual identity, and the other which lay hidden deep within me, the Christian. As this pain grew, I felt increasingly hopeless and depressed, yet outwardly I continued to conform to the politi-cally correct image of the "well-rounded" homosexual. I began believing that the hope I had once known in Christ was false, that it was nothing more than a cheap tribal feeling. One thing pre-vented the hidden Christian current within me from ceasing to flow: I still believed that Jesus was God. For this reason, I con-tinued to be troubled with guilt for not living according to Chris-tian standards. Additionally, I periodically talked to Jesus, though I never bothered waiting to hear His reply.

One night while coming home from a gay bar, I was walking up the stairwell of my apartment building, talking aloud to Jesus. I was a bit perturbed that I continued to sense God watching over me after I had obviously chosen a lifestyle against His will. Drunk-enly, I cried out to Him, "I would be better off if You just left me alone so that I could go on with my life unencumbered by this

Christian guilt left over from my teens." Then a verse from the Bible popped into my head: "Never will I leave you; never will I forsake you" (Hebrews 13:5).

As I reached the third floor, I decided that if God wasn't going to leave me alone, I should try leaving Him altogether. This idea had never crossed my mind before. Standing before the doors that opened to the hallway that led to my apartment, I said to Jesus, "That's it. I'm leaving You in this stairwell, and when I go through these doors into the hallway, I'll be free of You and these guilt feelings forever."

After walking through those doors and proceeding down the hallway toward my apartment, my eyes were opened to see literally hundreds of demons charging toward me. Never before had I seen anything quite like this, but I knew what they were. Terrified, I raced back into the stairwell, closed the doors behind me, and said, "I didn't mean it, Lord. I don't want to leave You; suffering with You is better than suffering without You."

I hesitantly opened the stairwell doors and peeked into the hallway. Seeing nothing, I cautiously walked down the hallway to my apartment door. Once inside, I locked the door behind me, went to bed, and tried to forget what had just happened.

From that incident I learned that God does not impose His will on us, nor does He hold us hostage. God holds every believer tightly in the palm of His hand, and though He will never let go, we have the freedom to choose to jump out. Moreover, Jesus teaches in Scripture that both He and the Father preserve believers in the faith and that no outside force, no matter how strong, can snatch us from His hand.

> I give them eternal life, and they shall never perish; no one can snatch them out of my hand. My Father, who has given them to me, is greater than all; no one can snatch them out of my Father's hand. (John 10:28, 29)

God in a Gay Bar

In addition to teaching part time, I also waited on tables at a restaurant in a Marriott Hotel. One evening several weeks later after finishing my shift, I took the subway to Copley Square. I stopped in the middle of the Square in front of Trinity Church—a glorious, mammoth building. Staring up at the starlit universe, I asked myself, "Where is God?" Leaving Trinity Church behind, I continued on through Copley Square, walked behind the John Hancock Tower, and followed a poorly lit narrow street that led to a gay bar I often patronized.

Once inside, I went to the main bar and ordered a vodka martini on the rocks. While sipping my drink, I took a long sweeping look at all the men in the bar. A hundred male bodies pulsated on the dance floor to a Michael Jackson tune. The sour smell of their perspiration pervaded the air. A short, overweight Latino man with a huge fan was doing a dance I assumed was native to South America. The dance floor was framed on two sides by long carpeted benchlike bleachers. Huge refrigerator-sized speakers at each end of the bleachers blared out music. Off to one end was a separate smaller barroom. Little tables surrounded by chairs filled this room, and men who did not like to dance conversed by shouting to each other over the loud music. In another corner stood several pool tables where black and Latino boys in their late teens congregated. A friend of mine used to call this area "Swoozie Land." This was some kind of racial slur.

The bar was supported by illusory pillars created by cigarette smoke trapped in solid beams of light shining from small powerful overhead lamps. In the many shadowy corners hid older homosexual men. Their eyes were glassed over and deeply empty. Hopelessly, they stared at the younger men in the bar. The younger gays, myself included, referred to these men as "trolls." Trolls were subhuman creatures who never saw the light of day. They lived in the night and were fed by the memories of their long lost youth. There were even special bars for trolls, called "wrinkle rooms." On a few occasions, my friend Bob and I went to one of these bars and entertained the trolls as we sang Broadway show tunes around the piano.

The glassed-over hopelessness in the eyes of the trolls grieved me. Still drinking my vodka martini, I thought, *Surely God loves these men. Surely God intends more for their lives than this.* Then, looking at my reflection in a nearby mirror, I asked myself, *Will my eyes one day be dark and empty like theirs?* Words from Scripture flowed through my head: "The eye is the lamp of the body. So, if your eye is sound, your whole body will be full of light; but if your eye is not sound, your whole body will be full of darkness. If then the light in you is darkness, how great is the darkness!" (Matthew 6:22, 23 RSV).

Deep in my gut a sinking feeling overtook me, and I began to descend into despair. Then coming from above me I heard a voice say, "You will help Me deliver these people." Thinking it was my sardonic friend Bob, I turned around expecting to find him standing behind me, gleaming from ear to ear with his naughty-boy smile. But he was not there. *Oh no,* I thought, *I'm hearing things.* Promptly, I ordered another vodka martini.

With a second drink in hand, I left the main bar and walked across the crowded dance floor. Trying to drown out that unwanted voice, I sat on one of the carpeted bleachers right next to a large speaker. With my ears pounding with music, I once again heard the voice, but now with more clarity than the first time: "YOU WILL HELP ME DELIVER THESE PEOPLE." I knew this was the voice of God. Fear gripped my heart.

Putting my untouched martini down on the bench, I stood up to leave. Then the music stopped. As I took my first step to cross the dance floor for the exit, every man on the dance floor moved away, like the parting of the Red Sea. Outside the bar a taxi waited. Holding open the passenger door, the driver asked me, "Need a ride, Buddy?"

"Yes."

He drove me home. Once in my apartment, I promptly blocked this out of my mind and went to sleep.

The next morning during breakfast, I kept thinking about what I had heard at the bar. Rationalizing it away, I decided a combination of tiredness and vodka had gotten the best of me. "Why would God speak to me?" I questioned. He had never spoken to me before; why should He now? Christianity was all behind me. For years I had been caught in the homosexuality-versus-Christianity vice-grip. That painful episode of my life was over, and I had barely escaped with my emotional and mental health. No more religion for this boy.

But I had not reckoned on the inexorable, irresistible love of God. He continued patiently arranging the circumstances of my life to show me the consequences of the way of life I had chosen. As each symptom of AIDS appeared, my fear and hopelessness increased. It became more and more difficult to hang on to the illusion of fulfillment in the gay utopia. So on that fateful night in Boston City Hospital when He offered me a choice, my resistance crumbled. I took hold of His hand and began walking out of darkness into His incredible freedom and light.

The Road to Repentance

After my release from the hospital, I telephoned my sister Annelyse in Milwaukee and told her about my miraculous physical healing. Annelyse had played a great role in my coming to Christ during my adolescence. She was at that time taking an adult Christian education class at her church, "Restoring Personal Wholeness Through Healing Prayer," taught by Leanne Payne.

A few weeks later, Annelyse wrote me a long letter, placed it within the pages of a copy of Leanne Payne's book, *The Broken Image*, and mailed it to me. Since I was open to the power of God to heal me physically, she reasoned that this was the time to inform me of His power to heal my sexuality. But I was not ready for that just yet.

When I received the package, I opened Leanne's book to the preface and read the opening paragraph where she calls homosexuality both a neurosis and a problem. Thinking myself to be a well-adjusted homosexual, I was offended. I shelved the book without finding the letter hidden between the pages.

Several months went by. One weekend I found myself home alone and ill with a severe cold. To a man who had come within moments of being diagnosed with AIDS, a simple cold was enough to send me into a frenzy of fear. As I lay there on my couch, wrapped in several blankets and filled with anxiety, I remembered that book, but I couldn't remember where I put it.

After searching for quite a while, I noticed the corner of the book hanging over the edge of the top of my wardrobe. As I reached up, the book fell, and Annelyse's letter fluttered to the floor.

Her letter, so full of love for me, prepared my heart to read Leanne's book. In the letter, she explained that God is present to me at all times, even to all my past moments, as if they were now, because He is outside of time; time is a created thing. As a result, He is able to heal all hurts no matter when they happened. Therefore, we are not hopelessly bound by those wounds and sins from the past that continue to shape us in our adult lives. Annelyse then asked for my forgiveness for any way in which she had failed to treat me with love and had judged me for my homosexuality. That perhaps was the key factor that motivated me to read Leanne's book.

I had great difficulty reading *The Broken Image*. Because I did not want to leave the homosexual lifestyle just yet, I would not allow myself to believe the healings documented within it. Though I knew that Jesus had healed me of my physical ailment a few months earlier, I was still ensnared in the current popular lie that homosexuality is an alternative lifestyle, not a neurosis that necessitates a cure. However, powerful truths in Leanne's book still broke through to me—all people bear wounds from broken relationships—relationships with God, with others, with themselves. There is no healing without the cross of Jesus. Forgiveness flows from His wounds.

I had many broken relationships, but one in particular was most pressing—the relationship with my father. The woundedness I felt from him was so great that it was as if he were a dark presence observing my every move, even though we lived a thousand miles apart. Following the examples in *The Broken Image*, I decided to begin praying daily and ask the Lord to show me any past events involving my father where I needed to forgive or be forgiven. Memories flooded to the fore, one after another. Many were too painful to face, but I found myself praying "healing-of-memories" prayers such as those described in *The Broken Image*. Never did I think that praying in this way would eventually lead me to repent of homosexuality as a sin or seek healing for it as a neurosis. I simply thought I was praying to be free of the negative influences from the past that still affected my life.

Praying regularly for the first time in over ten years, I became aware that not only was Jesus speaking to me, but also that He was trying to give me direction for my life. It was in prayer that I heard God tell me to take a teaching job at a small university in Ohio and turn down a job possibility in Montreal. Within six months, I moved from Boston, leaving behind gay friends and the gay nightlife, and found myself living in Kettering, Ohio.

During that first quarter at Wright State University in the autumn of 1983, loneliness overcame me. I had little opportunity to meet other gay people and missed my gay friends back east. Toward the end of the quarter, I became depressed. I began to realize that God was also asking me to choose between Himself and homosexuality. For the first time, I seriously considered the possibility that homosexuality could be reversed through faith in Jesus Christ. Up to this point, however, due to my involvement in the "politically correct" thinking characteristic of the homosexual lifestyle, I had never allowed myself the freedom to believe such an idea. (It's perfectly amazing how those who pride themselves on being "politically correct" do not allow themselves or others the intellectual freedom to explore all avenues of thought, such as the healing of homosexuality.) A day never went by that I did not think about the miraculous physical healing Jesus had done in me many months earlier.

As winter break approached, Annelyse called me. She said that Leanne Payne was going to repeat the class on personal wholeness at her church beginning the first Sunday in December.

"Mario, would you be willing to take the class while you're here for the holidays?"

I hesitated. Finally, I said, "Yes."

She replied, "Good. I already signed you up for it."

I was filled with anxiety when the day for the class came. The church met in the auditorium of an elementary school on Milwaukee's east side. As I neared the door to the room, fear and anxiety stirred so violently within that I became nauseous.

"Oh, Jesus, help me," I prayed. To my surprise, I saw a mental image of a large uncovered trash can filled with rotting garbage. As I continued to pray, I saw the lid of the trash can begin to move and cover the stinking, dark mess. Only a little sliver of the rim remained open. I felt that God was assuring me that He would only bring up those issues that I could deal with in the class. I had feared that if everything came up at once, I would break down completely. Looking back, I now realize that I was beginning to let down my defenses against accepting homosexuality as a neurosis. Feelings and depression that had been repressed for years were beginning to surface. I was on the verge of a nervous breakdown.

As I walked into the classroom, Leanne was already speaking. Annelyse had saved a seat for me in the back of the classroom and was beckoning to me. Once seated, I looked around the room, an old gymnasium. Leanne was teaching under a basketball hoop that was folded up toward the ceiling. She wore a white blouse with a plain black skirt. Over her shoulders hung a beautiful loosely woven shawl that looked handmade. My ears tuned into her words just as she was reading, with great joy, Psalm 139. She especially emphasized verses 13–16:

> For you created my inmost being; you knit me together in my mother's womb. I praise you because I am fearfully and wonderfully made; your works are wonderful, I know that full well. My frame was not hidden from you when I was made in the secret place. When I was woven together in the depths of the earth, your eyes saw my unformed body. All the days ordained for me were written in your book before one of them came to be.

She paused here, then said something to the effect, "Dear ones, God the Father has known you since before you were born. He takes great delight in being with His people. He took great delight in coming present to you, God incarnate through His Son Jesus. God is present to every painful memory that shapes you. He is present to heal every hurt in your life." I knew I was hearing truth as surely as I had when in first grade I learned that one plus one equals two. My eyes welled with tears, and I swallowed a big lump of pain trying to escape from my belly.

From then on, the pain within was so great that I heard little else. As Leanne continued teaching, occasionally I caught a word, and it sank in deeply. However, for the most part, all I heard was,

"Blah, blah, blah, blah, FATHER. Blah, blah, blah, FORGIVENESS. Blah, blah, blah, THE CROSS OF JESUS." I thought to myself, Is this lady speaking word-salad, or is it me? In hindsight, I now realize that the survival mechanism of denial allowed me to hear only those things my soul could comprehend.

Leanne encouraged all of us in her class to begin a prayer journal, which I did. She told us to write down all our thoughts before God, to dialogue with Him, and then to wait for that healing word that He would give. In the first entry of my prayer journal I wrote:

> Dec. 7, 1983
> There is some apprehension within me about changing something that progressed so naturally within my evolution into manhood. Although this may sound like pro-gay political defensive rhetoric, it is a real feeling inside too.
> But above all and beyond all, my faith in God and Jesus and the Spirit is my first concern. And I say it again, "I do not have faith on the premise that God will change me; it is because of my faith that I can consider the possibility that He will do so."

I still was not convinced that healing from homosexuality was possible, but I had come to the point in my relationship with God that I could no longer deny Him. Never again was I going to live life without God. If He wanted to change my homosexuality, I was willing to let Him. Toward that end, I agreed to do whatever He asked of me. And I was honest before God. A large part of me liked being gay. I enjoyed the fellowship in the gay lifestyle and the lustful gratification I experienced in homosexual encounters. Homosexuality was not disgusting to me; rather, much of it was pleasurable, and I wrote this out in my prayer journal.

The time in Milwaukee shed much light on the dark corners of my past—corners in which many painful childhood memories hid, memories I had previously worked hard to deny. I began to ask myself, If these painful memories have played a part in shaping my sexuality, how natural can homosexuality be? During that December, I took some steps to assist the healing God was trying to pour into me. I even stopped my sexual fantasy life and curbed the masturbation that went along with it, though this took immense effort and prayer.

Back in Ohio again for the new term at school, I became depressed. I faced not only terrible loneliness, but also all of the newly surfaced unresolved pain from within. Vaguely remembering the name of a church where one of my students, the only Christian in my class, attended, I decided to go to the evening service.

As I listened to the simple message of the gospel, the reasons for the development of my homosexuality crystalized in my mind. The book *The Broken Image*, some counsel from Annelyse's pastor—Dave Brown, Leanne's class, and now this simple preacher all pointed me in one direction—the cross of Jesus. It was now apparent to me that my homosexuality was nothing more than my sinful reaction to sins committed against me and to the wounding those sins had caused to my soul. Homosexuality was a defense my soul had erected to deal with the pain. For the first time, I saw that my homosexuality was also a sin that necessitated repentance. Just as the prodigal son at the pig trough "came to himself" (Luke 15:17 KJV), so too "I came to myself" as I faced the sins of the past, both mine and those of others, that had shaped me.

When the preacher gave the altar call for anyone who needed to be reconciled to God, I went forward, holding back tears. An associate pastor came to my side and whispered, "Do you know that your name is written in the Lamb's Book of Life?"

My throat was constricted with sorrow over my sin. My body was trembling at the presence of God in that place. I choked out, "No, I've committed too many sins."

"That doesn't matter; just repent of those sins." In saying this he ministered true grace to me.

With tears of sorrow pouring from my eyes, I repented of all my sins, including the sin of homosexuality.

Then this associate pastor said to me, "Now ask Jesus to show you the Lamb's Book of Life, and you'll see your name there written in His blood." And I saw it! That image of my name, Mario Bergner, written in red in the Book of Life sank so deep into my soul that tears of joy poured out from the center of my being. What happened next could only be considered a miracle.

The associate pastor asked, "Do you want to be filled with the Holy Spirit?"

"Sure," I said. I didn't even know you could ask for such a thing.

He called over some of the elders of the church. While some laid hands on me, others held my arms up, and then the associate pastor prayed, "Lord Jesus, come and fill this man with Your Holy Spirit."

Like a great rush of wind from Heaven, the Holy Spirit descended into the depth of my being. All the fear and dread lodged in my gut left me, and more tears of joy flowed from my eyes. A few moments later, a heavenly language of tongues welled up from within me. I spoke words of pure praise and adoration to God.

As I drove home that evening, the gnawing anxiety, the raw fear, and the clutter of confused thoughts that had plagued my mind for years were gone. I was at peace with God. Serenity bathed my soul. Not only had I received the forgiveness of sins and a powerful baptism in the Holy Spirit, but also I was delivered from an infestation of demons that had taken up residence in my body because of my sin.

That night, for the first time in ten years, I slept straight through until morning. When I woke up, I slowly got out of bed, went into the kitchen, fixed a pot of coffee, walked outside, stared at the blue morning sky, and still filled with deep peace I asked God, "Is this a dream?"

What happened to me over those eleven months, between being hospitalized in Boston and repenting at the little church in Ohio, was the completion of the conversion that had started in my adolescence. During that time the sinful circumstances of my life brought me to the absolute end of myself. Paradoxically, I was also being graciously wooed by Jesus into the Kingdom of God. These were the most painful eleven months of my life, as during this time God was working in me "a broken and contrite heart" (Psalm 51:17) to finally sacrifice up to Him at my repentance.

In Jesus' day a popular rabbinical teaching declared: "Great is repentance, for it brings healing upon the world."[1] I am grateful to God that during those eleven months He protected me from the foolish teaching that psychologizes all inner pain rather than properly naming some of it as sin. "For the time will come when men will not put up with sound doctrine. Instead, to suit their own desires, they will gather around them a great number of teachers to say what their itching ears want to hear" (2 Timothy 4:3). Some of this inner pain is the soul's quest to be free from sin. Unfortunately, many never gain the life-changing benefits that come when one deeply repents of sin and receives God's forgiveness.

Repentance at the cross of Jesus is the foundational healing for all who seek to be free from any life-controlling affliction. Repentance is the remedy the soul needs for primary release from pain, for only then can true healing follow. The cross of Jesus and the repentance it demands empowered me to fully disengage myself from my sinful past. No longer was my identity that of a homosexual. I was now free to embark, to cross over, onto the glorious road of identification with Christ. The healing work that Jesus had begun in me could now go on to completion.

Coming Out of Denial

Facing Evil and Rejection

Death and Destruction lie open before the
Lord—how much more the hearts of men!

Proverbs 15:11

All in the Family

My father was born in a beautiful little town in the Saxony region of Germany. He was the last of thirteen children raised by a cruel, authoritarian father and a meek, loving mother. Never once did I hear my father tell any story about his father that contained a kind word. It is obvious to me that Grandfather never honored my father as a person and never affirmed him as a man. Consequently, my father could not in turn affirm me as a man. The sins of my grandfather against my father continue to shape him to this day.

My father has yet to find freedom from the evil effects of growing up in Nazi Germany. His personal beliefs are stained with the anti-Semitism and white supremacist ideas he learned in school. From 1945–48, the Americans held him as a prisoner of war. In one of many American prison camps along the banks of the Rhine River, he lived for over a year outdoors in a chicken-wire pen, sleeping in a dirt hole, nightly hearing the cries of hundreds of his fellow countrymen as they died of starvation. Somehow, in the providence of God, he barely managed to hang on. Then the Americans delivered him to the French. Relocated to a prisoner of war camp in Soulac, France, he arrived weighing about eighty pounds.

My father's upbringing and his imprisonment shaped him into something God never intended him to be. His brokenness caused overwhelmingly sinful behavior toward his family. Often he seemed unable to control himself and was at the mercy of deep-seated pain, hatred, and anger lodged in his soul. I too was headed in a similar direction, but Jesus entered in and broke the pattern of the sins of the fathers being visited upon the children (see Exodus 20:5).

My father needed to control those around him. Failing to treat others as persons to be honored, he related to those closest to him merely as extensions of himself. The love he expressed toward us was not affirming, but diseased, a love that knew no proper boundaries between himself and us. He manipulated and controlled his wife and children into doing things which to him were signs that we loved him. His demands were so confused and devouring that all who came within his personal world ended up feeling defiled by his manipulative ploys. I finally came to realize there was no pleasing him, no convincing him that he was ever truly loved. In order to break free from his crushing control, I permanently left home at age twenty, exasperated and embittered.

My father knows what it is to be both victim and perpetrator. He was and still is a broken man in need of Christ's redeeming love. I struggled for many years *after* forgiving him, trying to make sense out of his evil and sinful behaviors against me, my sisters, and my mother. All the more confusing to me was that on rare occasions he would be gentle and kind. His love for nature, gardening, and animals was something I rarely saw in the fathers of my childhood friends.

My mother grew up in the wine country of southern France. She was the second oldest of six girls raised by a cold, distant mother and an affectionate, though alcoholic, father. Five of the six girls married alcoholics. My mother is the only one who did not; however, my father's problems easily matched those of the person suffering from alcoholism. He constantly used mocking and degrading remarks to keep her in subjection to him.

After the war, the French people branded Mother a collaborationist for giving birth to a half-French, half-German child, my eldest sister Maryse. They treated both her and her daughter in cruel and dehumanizing ways.

Though my mother clearly loved us, at times she yielded to the evil affecting my father and failed to protect her children or indeed to exercise her rights as a human being. She excused my father's behavior, reminding us "of the hard life he had suffered" or that he had been brutally treated while a prisoner of war. Both of these were true, but neither are excuses for inexcusable behavior.

My mother did not know how to maintain proper personal boundaries between herself and others. She often confided in me in ways inappropriate for a mother to share with her son. An unhealthy bond grew between us, contributing to the homosexual neurosis developing in me. This unhealthy attachment, what some psychologists call "emotional incest," constitutes a role reversal between child and parent. In my case I became a surrogate husband to my mother. According to Hemfelt, Minirth, and Meier:

> Here is where a loving relationship between parent and child has somehow been turned upside down. In the parent's mind (and rarely consciously considered) is the thought, "I don't care much for my spouse, but I have this child, whom I love more than life itself."[1]

Eventually I needed prayer to get an emotional divorce from my mother in order to become healthy. Finally, I had to establish proper emotional boundaries between us in order to remain healthy.

Deprivation in the Home

Both my mother and father experienced deep losses before they married. My mother saw her father's business bombed and destroyed twice during World War II. My father once told me that on the morning he was taken, against his will, into the German military, it was like being ripped prematurely from his mother's womb. He lost seven brothers and sisters in the war. Both my parents were in their teens when the war began. They lost their childhoods, family members, their countries as they knew them, their homes, and their firstborn son. In short, they lost life as they knew it.

The damage to a personality from such deep losses is beyond description. When persons with such deprivations marry, they try to regain what they lost by starting anew. The new family becomes the means for healing the pain of the past. They make incredible sacrifices for this family. My father worked two and three jobs to pull us out of poverty. By sheer will, he built a successful business, made a good income, built a large home in the suburbs, and sent his children to college. He was determined to give us what had been denied to him. Both he and my mother tried their hardest to give us the very best life possible. I love and respect them for that.

But deep within them, through no fault of their own, the past deprivations had left a great emptiness. This emptiness prevented them from being emotionally present to their children even when most needed. My parents could not give us what they themselves lacked. So we too experienced deep deprivation.

Moreover, we faced overt evil and rejection in the home and the lack of simple things necessary to healthy childhood development. As a family we rarely had mealtimes together. Our parents never read to us. They did not treat us with dignity and respect as little persons growing into individuals. When we were hurt, we rarely ran to Mommy or Daddy for comfort. Sometimes we children ran to each other. Most times we retreated into ourselves.

There were seven people in our family. We could all be home at the same time, yet each be utterly alone. We never made the proper familial attachments necessary for healthy emotional development. We were "disrelated" from each other. Only in times of extraordinary crisis would we pull together as a family. But for the ordinary day-to-day struggles of life, we were not there for each other.

Dick Keyes in his excellent book *Beyond Identity* writes:

> We grow as individuals and find our identity not by ourselves but in the context of many different relationships—with parents, brothers and sisters, older relatives, spouses, children, associates and friends.[2]

In these primary family relationships the sense of self develops. Deprived of these needed relationships, children may never have a solid sense of being at the inner core of their personality. They look to other people to tell them who they are. My parents tried to get a sense of self from their children. The homosexual, insecure in his gender identity, attempts to attach himself to another of the same sex in an attempt to attain an identity.

Failure to meet a child's basic emotional needs brings on a kind of "deprivation neurosis," an intense inner pain that drives the person to try to make up the deficit. The child never made a proper attachment to another person and consequently does not know the peace of well-being in the love of another. A pervasive sense of inner emptiness results. Trying to fill this emptiness may become the driving force in this person's life. He or she may form inordinate attachments to people, objects, or substances. This emptiness may also elicit deep feelings of anxiety. When this is the case, alleviating the anxiety becomes extremely important in the life of the person suffering from deprivation.

Deprivation is hallmarked by powerful negative feelings which may override the good of reason. Envy, hatred, anger, and rejection may be the only feelings the person has. He or she tends to operate subjectively from these feelings. Unlike the person who is able to repress or shut off his feelings through intellectual and other defenses, the deprived person is unable to repress the negative feelings. To compensate, he or she may develop addictions that provide pleasure—to alcohol, food, cigarettes, or sex. As adults, some persons with deprivation can only feel sexual desires. Consequently, they eroticize all their relationships.

The person with deprivation often feels intellectually incompetent. Proper intellectual functioning, such as operating at one's academic potential in school, can rarely happen apart from a secure emotional base. When the home environment does not produce this security, most children consistently perform below their ability in school. Such was the case in our home. None of us did well in school until we left home and established an emotional support system with friends or spouses to sustain us through our education. The following quote from *Healing the Unaffirmed* by Dr. Conrad Baars and Dr. Anna Terruwe parallels my own struggle with intellectual pursuits:

> A girl with a severe deprivation neurosis always felt that she was incapable of doing anything well, in spite of the fact that she was an unusually gifted person in almost every field. She was of superior intelligence, most artistic, and skillful with her hands. Yet her work was never completed; when she began something, she would give it up after a while with the excuse that she "would not be able to finish it anyway!" However, after a year of treatment, she outgrew her fears and was able to persevere in her efforts. Now she succeeded in everything she undertook. She told us then that she had never wanted to learn before because she feared that if she were to try anything, it would turn out to be a failure.[3]

Only after I began receiving healing and affirmation through the church, Leanne Payne, and the team at Pastoral Care Ministries did I dare to finish my undergraduate degree. Leanne was a great cheerleader on my behalf during this time. She lovingly exhorted me to continue in my studies, assuring me that with the help of God I could complete the education I had started years earlier.

Deprivation in a person may also manifest in what Drs. Baars and Terruwe call "willed rapport." Because the person lacks the deep positive emotions normally acquired in the context of a loving and secure family environment, he or she cannot form friendships based on positive feelings. Therefore, many of the relationships are willed friendships.

> Friendship supposes a mutual exchange of feelings, being emotionally tuned in on one another. But this is precisely what is lacking on the part of the deprivation neurotic. . . . Deprivation neurotics may be capable of establishing superficial contacts with acquaintances, even good acquaintances, but these never develop into emotionally satisfying friendships. It is therefore not surprising that all deprivation neurotics say that they feel lonely.[4]

I certainly did. For ten years I moved from city to city. It was easy to leave one place and go to the next because I had no strong, committed relationships, other than family ties and childhood friends. Also, good social skills enabled me to initiate and sustain superficial friendships easily. Once in a new locale, I could quickly gather around me many "new friends." But I have not retained one friend made during those years. By contrast, today my friendships are lasting, deeply committed relationships built on mutual vulnerability and trust.

Still another manifestation of deprivation is supersensitivity. The underlying negative feelings in a person with deprivation are always unconsciously being introduced into their present relationships. The slightest negative word from someone may elicit deep feelings of rejection or anger. At other times, the underlying feeling of rejection is projected into relationships and situations where no actual rejection is occurring. As a result, those with deprivation often feel rejected when no actual rejection has occurred.

My deep fear of rejection caused me to keep people at arms' length. While I could be entertaining in social contexts, I did not let anyone really know me. If someone got too close, a protective wall of invulnerability came down. On numerous occasions acquaintances commented on how aloof and detached I seemed.

Deprivation can also manifest itself in paranoid feelings. I do not mean paranoia in the sense of spinning a delusional system of thought—such as the individual who believes the CIA is plotting to kill him. I mean paranoia in the sense of a deep suspicion of others based on an inability to trust them. The person with deprivation never experienced the deep trusting relationships with primary caregivers in the home. As a result, he or she enters all new relationships with mistrust. When conflicts arise in existing relationships, the person with deprivation may overreact and attribute nonexistent motives to others.

Coming Out of Denial

Painful, secretive stories of the horrors of war, which everyone knew not to bring up, filled my childhood home. Some nights I was startled out of my sleep by the sound of my father screaming in agony, followed by my mother's voice gently awakening him from yet another nightmare of his imprisonment. In the course of family life my father would frequently erupt like a volcano filled with hot molten anger, often for no apparent reason. He matches perfectly the diagnostic criteria for Post-traumatic Stress Disorder.[5] The wounding effects of war were ever present in our home.

The unhealthy patterns of relating found in the dysfunctional family and the survival roles of rescuer, lost child, mascot, and scapegoat all emerged within our home. These roles which my sisters and I took on enabled us to function within the chaos of home life. Nevertheless, they had a detrimental side. We failed to see the behavioral patterns attached to the roles as the result of sin (disorder) in the home, and we brought these dysfunctional behaviors into our adult Christian lives.

Like most children from dysfunctional homes, we coped with the intense pain by going into denial. Denial could be defined as the conscious or unconscious decision to refuse to face the reality about something. When immediate healing for such pain is not available, denial can prevent one from having to wander through life a hurting, useless mess. In our family the disorder was so obvious that we simply could not deny certain things. However, we were truly successful at denying the degree to which the home was dysfunctional and the degree to which we were personally affected by this unhealthy environment.

I needed to come out of denial in seasons, as I could not possibly face everything at once. The most difficult part for me was coming to acknowledge the degree to which my father had chosen to side with evil. I could admit some of his evil behaviors, but never all of them. The palpable presence of evil filled our home.

Dr. Scott Peck's book *People of the Lie* greatly helped me to understand the psychology of human evil—both its devastating effects on my father and its existence in the depths of my own heart. The introduction to the book is entitled "Handle with Care." Dr. Peck warns his readers that some may misuse the information in his book to harm others. He cautions:

> Evil people are easy to hate. But remember Saint Augustine's advice to hate the sin but love the sinner. Remember when you recognize an evil person that truly, "There, but for the grace of God, go I."[6]

I struggle with whether it is ever correct to label another human being hopelessly evil. Redemption through the cross has come even to the most vile of sinners. And in every person, no matter how sinful, remain the veiled vestiges of what it means to be created in the image of God. Throughout history, the great saints in Christendom have taught that no matter what a person has done, the cross of Christ waits to be applied to their circumstances. It is written of Catherine of Siena:

> Great as was her horror of sin, she was never known to shrink from the vilest of sinners whilst there was any hope of winning them to better things. She saw the possibilities that lay hidden under the most unpromising exterior, and it was her unwavering belief in the existence of that "better self" in human nature, however fallen, that so often gave people strength and courage to overcome the "worse."[7]

The Gift of Divine Objectivity

Fortunately for me, during this time of coming out of denial, I was surrounded by loving Christians both at my local church and through my work at Pastoral Care Ministries. These dear friends exhorted me to face objectively the evil in my father, to love the *real* person in him, whom Jesus died to redeem, and to pray for his salvation. In order to do this, I needed to receive the "gift of divine objectivity."

Leanne Payne's book *Crisis in Masculinity* was exceptionally helpful to me in this area. She writes:

> A child can seldom differentiate between its parents as persons and their sinfulness, sickness, or weakness. The parent and the behavior appear to the child to be one. Later, in order to be free, the son or daughter has to separate the two. He has to forgive the sin and accept the sinner. To do this, he or she must gain what I have come to call the gift of divine objectivity. . . .
>
> It is a tough task to face the darkness that is in one's own parents. But through prayer, the obstacles to this facing and naming can be overcome. And it is only in this way that these persons can begin to get their identities separated from both their parents and past situations and go on to truly forgive. In this way, too, they can begin to take full responsibility for their own grievous reactions to the problem. They can fully confess and repent of their own sins in the matter.[8]

As healing has come into my heart, I have been freed to love my father objectively without expecting anything in return. On occasions when the "better self" in my father emerges, I am able to celebrate and affirm that in him.

I treasure in my heart a memory from a visit to my parents' home when my father's "better self" emerged for an entire afternoon. After we had lunch on the patio, my father, nature lover that he is, suggested we go for a walk in the park nearby. As we started off, he gently took my mother's hand and swung their arms as they walked along. Public displays of affection between him and my mother have always been rare. Once in the park, he informed me that if we followed the trail, we would see a mother duck and her six ducklings in the creek. Indeed, we ran into the happy family of ducks, at which point my father commanded us to be quiet lest we disturb them. Toward the end of our walk, we climbed over a huge hill on which I used to go sledding during the long, snowy Wisconsin winters. Next to the hill was a railroad track. In the distance we could hear the whistle of an oncoming train.

"Let's wait for the train to pass," my father said. When it came, my mother and father together began counting the cars, each in their native language. At the end she called out the number of the cars in French at the same time he called out the number in German. Much to their delight, they came up with the same number. They laughed together.

Unfortunately, the false, prideful "worst self" most often reigns in my father—the self that so wounded me as a child. Between that part of my father and myself I have had to establish some very clear boundaries so as not to let the evil in him hurt me any more. In doing this I honor my father by not giving him the occasion to sin against me.

Failed Attempts at Understanding Evil

Until I received this gift of divine objectivity, I fell into two extremes in attempting to comprehend the evil in my father, in the circumstances of my parents' lives, and in our home. These two extremes were intellectualization and superspirituality. These were defenses I used along with denial to control the inner pain.

While stuck in intellectualization, I would endlessly play over in my mind the events of the past, especially those terrible memories of the home that seemed so senseless and cruel. I tried to understand what psychological injuries might cause a person to behave so monstrously against another human being. Thinking that insight into the horrors of World War II would supply me with answers, I read several books on the subject. Shortly before my return to Christ, I read Viktor Frankl's book *Man's Search for Meaning*. It spoke to me one great truth—man's primary hope for survival lies in his relationships. Many who survived the concentration camps of Nazi Germany lived for the day they would be reunited with those they loved. For some, just the image of a loved one held deep within the heart was enough to nourish and strengthen the will to endure.

After coming back to Christ, I attempted to interpret the evil I saw in my father, in myself, and in the world from a purely spiritual perspective. Now I was apt to explain my father's evil behaviors (and those of my past) by attributing them exclusively to demonic influences. I even wondered at one point if Hitler had been the devil incarnate.

But this view excused the evil in humanity by shifting the blame to Satan. While we can acknowledge that Satan introduced evil into this world, we cannot blame him for the human choice to follow that evil. In blaming Satan, one fails to call man into accountability and repentance before God.

I knew that "The reason the Son of God appeared was to destroy the devil's work" (1 John 3:8b). While the Bible does not explain how God can be both good and sovereign in the face of the world's evil, it does give us the divine remedy for evil. Moreover, it gives us four accounts of this great remedy—the Gospels of Matthew, Mark, Luke, and John. As I sat at the foot of the cross in prayer, I realized that the evil in humanity and in the world really did necessitate God becoming man, dying on a tree to conquer evil, and taking all the sin of the world into Himself.

In my futile quest to comprehend evil, I felt at times as if my mind were suspended between sanity and insanity. In those moments when I feared that life was just a cruel joke or that my healing would never be completed, my heart was nourished and strengthened by the image of Christ on the cross. Then my prayer was simply to see Jesus hanging on the cross, dying to take the sins of the world into His body. Sometimes I would just pray His holy name over and over, "Jesus, Jesus, Jesus . . ." until my soul was comforted. There is power in the name of the Lord.

On other occasions I would go to a Catholic church, sit in the back pew, and look up at the huge crucifix hanging above the altar, letting that image of Jesus on the cross minister to me the reality of His redemptive work. Just as the image of a loved one sustained prisoners in the face of the evil of Nazi concentration camps, so the image of Jesus nourished and healed me while my body and soul shook with pain over the evil that dominated my childhood home.

Corrie and Betsie ten Boom, along with their father and brother, were part of the resistance movement in Holland. They hid Jews from the Nazis and helped them escape to freedom. In 1944 the entire family was arrested, and Corrie and Betsie were sent to Ravensbruck concentration camp. Ninety-six thousand women died at Ravensbruck. Betsie ten Boom was one of them. But until her dying day, Betsie had a saying about Jesus that encouraged many in their faith and helped sustain them through the horrors of that place: "There is no pit so deep that He is not deeper still."[9]

Before the cross in prayer, I could ask God all the why questions those who suffer ask. "Why do you make me look at injustice? Why do you tolerate wrong?" (Habakkuk 1:3). One day in prayer, I was reminded that Jesus on the cross also asked God a why question: "My God, my God, why have you forsaken me?" (Mark 15:34). It was then I realized that the Father did not answer Jesus' question (nor did God answer Habakkuk's). But three days later God responded by resurrecting Jesus from the dead. We may not receive the answers to our why questions, but we shall receive comfort for our pain through the resurrection power of Jesus, available to us in prayer.

In the end I learned to concentrate on the remedy and ask the more important how questions. "How in this circumstance, Lord Jesus, can I apply the healing power of the cross?" The answer was to look up and out of myself, in the midst of my pain, and hurt with my eyes fixed on Christ, risen from the dead, victorious over sin and evil.

No Room at the Inn

Widespread information on the dysfunctional family has given many people truth that has set them free. The negative side to this plethora of information is that it tends to trivialize the trauma of growing up in a dysfunctional home by constructing a paradigm that fits so many families. We may overlook the fact that each family has its own unique history, and no family should ever be viewed as just another dysfunctional family.

Only in prayer does God reveal how unique each family system really is. No two are alike. The singular suffering and deprivation within my family history no psychological system could ever address. Only the all-encompassing applicability of the cross could heal it. I did not understand the part a deep sense of rejection, traced back to my parents' past in war-torn Europe, played in my family's dysfunction. All this became clear to me, one insight after another, as I prayed.

One weekend several friends and I went to a healing conference at College Hill Presbyterian Church in Cincinnati, Ohio. In preparation for this weekend retreat we worked through a booklet called *Breaking Free from the Past*, written by Dr. Gary R. Sweeten.[10] For two months we followed the exercises that included exploration of one's family history. By the time we gathered for the retreat, we each had a pretty good idea of what our own family history was.

The format involved breaking into small groups and praying for each other for freedom from destructive things in the past. Prayer for each person lasted for about an hour and a half. Late Saturday afternoon my turn came. Between our arrival on Friday night and Saturday afternoon, God had been reminding me of the many painful stories from the past that my family had always avoided talking too much about. Now twenty-six years of avoiding these family stories seemed to me to be summed up in one theme: "No room at the inn."

The facilitator of my small group said, "It's your turn, Mario."

Holding back tears, I replied, "Yes, I know. I can't say it." My throat was so choked with pain I couldn't get the words out.

Dolores, a woman from my home church who was in this group, lovingly encouraged me. "Yes, you can, Mario. We're here for you, and so is Jesus."

I simply said, "No room at the inn." Then I began to weep bitterly.

"What do you mean by that?" someone asked.

"That's the story of my family. We've been in search of a place to call home, but we never find it. When I was seven years old, my sister Maryse mentioned my deceased brother Karl in passing to my mother. I had never heard his name spoken in our home before. My father went into a rage and screamed, "Those French doctors killed him. They wouldn't give him the proper medication."

I remembered my father screaming about many things that I knew were outright lies. Whether the doctors were remiss or not, I cannot know for sure, but I believed my father about this.

"Can you forgive those French doctors for that, Mario?" someone in the group asked me.

"No, I can't."

"Let Christ forgive them through you."

So in faith I released forgiveness to the doctors who had improperly treated my brother, the infant of a hated German, saying, "In Jesus' name, I forgive you."

Then an old photograph of my parents standing outside a dirt mound with a door in it came to my remembrance. Due to this photograph, I believed that my mother and father lived in an old bomb shelter that had been converted into apartments after World War II. In my heart, I believed my parents could not find any better housing in France after the war, primarily because they were a German-French couple.

"They lived in an old bomb shelter in the south of France. That's not a home," I cried out bitterly. As I wept, several people comforted me in Christ's name. The pain grew worse.

At one point my father had returned to Germany to look for a place where we could settle. He went to Passau, a lovely little village in the German Alps, but no apartments were available. The war had left much of Germany and Europe with a serious housing shortage. There was no room for us in Germany.

"My father even went back to his own country to find us a home. There was no room for us there either." My throat grew tighter.

Another photograph came up from my heart—this one from a collection of photographs in *Life* magazine. It depicted a young French woman with her head shaved. She carried a baby. The caption had read: "The shame of a female collaborationist, shorn in punishment, is reflected in the face of this [French] mother as she carries her German-fathered child through the streets to the taunts of her neighbors."

I remembered my mother telling me years earlier, "The French were cruel to Maryse and me. Several times they spat on us and urinated on us as I walked through the streets with her in my arms."

My body convulsed with pain at this picture and at my mother's words, and several people had to hold me down.

"They spat and urinated on my mother and my sister."

"Who?"

"Their own people. I hate the French."

"Can you forgive them?"

"No, and I don't want to."

"Let Christ forgive them through you."

I knew that if I did not let Christ's forgiveness flow through me to the French people, the hatred and anger in my body would eventually kill me. So in faith I spoke out. "I forgive the French people."

Then I remembered the first memory I have of my father. My family immigrated to Canada in the early 1950s to begin a new life and escape the painful past in Europe. I was born in Canada. In this memory, I was about three. I was swinging on the swing set my father had made in the back yard of our home in Thet Ford Mines, Quebec. My father came running home with his leg all bloody. I think he had been beaten up at work. Many French-Canadians resented my father because he was a hard worker, and they rejected us because of my parents' mixed marriage. Then I remembered my father saying, "We left Canada because the French-Canadians were going to treat Mario the way the French had treated Karl." Whether this was true or not (or just my father's paranoia rooted in his unhealed hurts from Karl's death), I do not know. But I had believed this since childhood.

I told those praying for me, "We left Canada because my father feared for my well-being. We were not welcome there."

"Can you forgive the Canadian people?"

I knew I must, so in Christ's name, once again I forgave.

Then came the most painful memory. When I was four years old, my family immigrated to the United States. We moved to Milwaukee when I was five years old and lived in an immigrant neighborhood on the west side.

One Sunday afternoon our family went to a department store. Upon leaving the store, my father noticed several older teenage boys tampering with our car. He ran over to them and in his thick German accent calmly told them to leave the car alone. They exchanged harsh words, and as the boys walked away, one shouted to my father, "Why don't you go back to your own country?"

My father's voice choked with pain, and in his thick German accent he weakly said, "Dis is my country too." There were tears in his eyes, and I saw him swallow a large lump of rejection and pain. Moments later in the car his pain came out in an eruption of hot anger against us. But I know he wasn't angry with us; he was in pain. Now I know that his anger is a reaction to his pain.

In the ride back to our flat, I thought to myself, We don't belong here. We had always talked about Americans as "them." We were Europeans with no place to call home. I hated Americans.

"No room in the inn," I cried. "No room in the inn. Just like Mary and Joseph, we have no place to call home. The French, the Germans, the Canadians, and the Americans all rejected us." I wanted to die and be with Jesus so I could finally be home.

Then one woman prayed an atonement prayer. It went something like this: "Dear Lord Jesus, I confess the sins of America against the Bergner family. Mario, can you forgive us Americans, here with you, for the sins of our country against your family?"

"In Jesus' name I do forgive you." By this time I was clear on one thing—forgiveness is an act of the will and is only possible when the will is aligned with God, the source of all forgiveness.

Then someone prayed for my heart to be healed of all the rejection that had so shaped my family and me. It was as if the sins of rejection lodged in my family history for decades had been constricting my soul, like a snake slowly killing its prey. In this prayer, at that very moment, the light of Christ's healing forgiveness entered my heart. The snake of rejection was loosened from me. The love of Jesus entered in and bound up the broken pieces of my heart and revived me. My desire to die left.

I tell you the truth, whatever you bind on earth will be bound in heaven, and whatever you loose on earth will be loosed in heaven. Again, I tell you that if two of you on earth agree about anything you ask for, it will be done for you by my Father in heaven. For where two or three come together in my name, there am I with them. (Matthew 18:18–20)

Because I had internalized the rejection in my family's past, up to that point in my life, I had habitually expected others to reject me. That expectation was a self-fulfilling prophecy and drew their rejection. Now for the first time I broke free from the sense of rejection that had shaped me. I became able to receive the love of others, from both men and women. Moreover, this healing freed me to begin to love others unconditionally, even in the face of actual rejection.

Self-Pity, Grief, and Envy

If we do not receive the gift of divine objectivity, we will continue looking to our parents for the love they failed to give us when we were children. We will not realize that they probably are as broken, maybe even as deprived, today as they were back then. In addition, we may fail to take responsibility for our childish and sinful reactions to the deprivation of our dysfunctional families. When this is the case, we see ourselves only as helpless victims. Consequently, we may get caught in the mode of the "self-pitying, whining and complaining child." Christian psychologist Gerard van den Aardweg writes:

> People with neurotic complaining tendencies sometimes maintain an attitude of reproach for what their parents have inflicted on them. One must realize that this may be yet another kind of complaining. Moreover, that prolonged complaining about the parents—of whom the complainer sees himself as the victim—is nearly always based on an unrealistic view of the parents. The complaining child's view of his parents is by definition a child's view, therefore one determined by ego-centered feelings. It needs correction if the person is to be more mature emotionally.[11]

As the voice of the complaining child emerged from within me, I wrote down all his negative and self-pitying beliefs in my prayer journal. In the process the real pain in which this immature child was rooted began to come forward. It was the grief of not ever having had a childhood.

This grief came fully to the surface as I saw healthy fathers relating to their sons within the Christian community. At first I envied those sons for having what I so desperately wanted. However, I confessed my sin of envy up to God and stopped wallowing in pity for the hurt little boy inside me. As I allowed myself to hurt before Jesus, to cry out to Him, to be in pain, the healing began to come.

This grief lasted for several months. Again the image of Jesus dying on the cross to take all the sin and pain of a broken, fallen world into His body was my sole comfort. I had a place to go with my pain. Toward the end of this period, another form of grief surfaced—grief over my sin. For four days I grieved intensely over the fact that I had sinned against my own body and against God with my past homosexual activity.

"There you will remember your conduct and all the actions by which you have defiled yourselves, and you will loathe yourselves for all the evil you have done. You will know that I am the LORD, when I deal with you for my name's sake and not according to your evil ways and your corrupt practices, O house of Israel," declares the Sovereign LORD. (Ezekiel 20:43, 44)

The line between self-pity and grief is not always easy to draw. However, the Rev. Clay McLean has set out six major differences between the two.

SELF-PITY

1. Destructive
2. Weak and whiny; never makes a clear statement of truth
3. Circular and descending

GRIEF

1. Healing
2. Strengthening and verbal; makes clear statements about legitimate losses and related feelings
3. Looks up and out of self and focuses on God

4. Does not do the basics of survival—no prayer, no listening to God, or dealing with basic issues	4. Does the basics; interacts with God, self, and others in a mature way
5. Dramatizes the past	5. Real communication of pain to self, God, and trusted friends
6. Collects wounds	6. Objectifies wounds without denying them

Self-pity is part of the practice of the presence of the "old man," the carnal self, whereas grieving is the capacity to hurt, all the while practicing the presence of God. To grieve out one's pain is a legitimate need for the wounded person, and the grace and permission to do so must be given to him or her. Like the psalmists or Job, every Christian must embrace true redemptive suffering before God.

Barriers to Healing

In the last ten years much has been written about the negative effects of growing up in a dysfunctional home. Unfortunately, some of this information has turned into psychological buzzwords that fail to heal and only succeed in labeling. While teaching and ministering to large groups, we find two common reactions to this information emerging, reactions that are barriers to healing.

Some under the direction of self-help groups have descended into the mode of the self-pitying, angry inner child. Though these fellow Christians may have gained much intellectual insight, their outlook on healing has become subjectively man-centered and not objectively God-centered. They are always digging for that next memory from their childhood to be revealed so they may have another reason to be angry. Once confronted about this tendency, they are grateful for the exhortation to take the good which they have received from such groups and to rise up out of their anger and objectify it in God's healing presence.

Conversely, it is equally common to find fellow Christians who disregard all psychological insight as anti-Christian. They spiritualize their past hurts and are quick to give to God problems He intends *them* to work out before Him. When asked about their childhood homes, they often reply, "Oh, it was terrible, but I've just given it to the Lord." However, their lives verify that they are still living under the negative effects of growing up in such an environment. Their trust in Jesus is good and correct, but they do not allow Him to come present to the heart in such a way as to reveal its wounds and heal them. Their "faith" then becomes another defense they use to remain in denial.

Christians who desire to be whole persons, that is to be mature in Christ, cannot afford to ignore the truths revealed by the relatively new information on the dysfunctional family. They are desperately in need of St. Augustine's advice: "Every good and true Christian should understand that wherever he may find truth, it is his Lord's."[12] Those who continue in ignorance of these new-found concepts are like the Israelites in Hosea's time who were "destroyed from lack of knowledge" (Hosea 4:6).

During the time Jesus was healing me of homosexuality, I found myself in both camps. While still in the glow of that powerful infilling of the Holy Spirit I received at the little church in Ohio, I was apt to spiritualize problems that God had no intention of taking away other than through redemptive suffering (my grieving and hurting before Him).

Once in touch with the pain, revealed by the insights I received from solid teaching on the dysfunctional family, I was apt to wallow in my anger and self-pity and fail to look up and out of myself and see Jesus. Fortunately, I was surrounded by loving, mature Christians who helped me when I was stuck in one of these two common extremes of wallowing in immature anger or spiritualizing away my problems.

I suspect that some of the readers of this book may find themselves caught in one of these extremes. And I would urge that neither spiritualizing nor self-pity be allowed to deny Christ access to the pain He died to redeem.

3

Disordered Love

The Development of Homosexuality

Be merciful to me, O Lord, for I am in distress;
my eyes grow weak with sorrow, my soul and
body with grief.

Psalm 31:9

Splitting Off from the Masculine

Unlike many children, I never wanted to imitate my father because I never saw in him qualities I admired. Not only did he fail to affirm me as a man, through emotional abuse he denigrated my emerging masculinity. So I repressed my masculinity, simply detaching from all that my father literally was to me. I actually remember making an inner vow never to become like him.

This vow and detachment from my father eventually generalized to all that he represented to me, including all other men. In my deep heart or inner being, my personality became split off from symbols of masculinity altogether. I did not doubt my biological sex, but I never felt that I was masculine.

Leanne Payne in her book *Crisis in Masculinity* tells the story of Richard, a man whose brokenness was so similar to mine that wherever his name appears in the quote below, I have substituted my own:

> What is it like to be alienated from an important part of oneself—from one's gender identity, with all its powerful archetypal symbols in the deep mind and heart? Psychologically, for [Mario] to be split off from his masculinity meant he was separated from the power to see and accept himself *as a man.* His inner vision of himself was sadly wanting. Like a gap-toothed grin, his perception of himself held gaping dark spaces. Within his heart there were no pictures of himself as a man and as a person in his own right. Such symbolic, as well as more realistic, images of oneself are taken for granted and are largely unnoticed by the person secure in his gender identity. But inside [Mario] there was a peculiar void, a nothingness that he attempted to fill with an unhealthy fantasy life. This fantasy life, as well as the images that welled up from his unhealed psyche, provided symbolic pictures of his gender confusion.[1]

Of the "images that welled up" from my unhealed and wounded psyche, three stand out to me. Around age five I became aware of a deep discomfort within myself toward my own sex. My fear of my father was growing, as was my sense of deep rejection by him. The heart has the ability to economically contain in a single symbol intense inner pain. My heart reduced masculinity and my deep alienation from it to one single symbol—men's feet. They fascinated me—unnaturally so. Coupled with this fascination was a sense of shame—my response to my sense of rejection from my father. Dr. Ruth Tiffany Barnhouse in her book, *Homosexuality: A Symbolic Confusion*, states that foot fetishes are common in dysfunctions of male sexuality.[2] I did not, however, have a full-blown foot fetish insofar as mine was not linked to a genital response.

Several years later, at around age ten, another symbol of masculinity replaced my fascination with men's feet. My family was preparing to move from the city to the suburbs. Just before moving, I planted the seed of a maple tree next to the base of a street lamp. After moving to the suburbs, I had repeated dreams of that maple seed growing so fast and so tall that it knocked over the street lamp. Even while awake, I was overcome with fear and guilt for having planted that maple seed.

At the first opportunity, I went back to our old house in the city to see if the maple tree had indeed knocked over the light. Of course it hadn't. Once again, my heart was economically containing in one symbol deep inner conflict. The tree and street lamp were both symbols of the masculine to me, and the fear of the maple tree growing and knocking down the lamp post was my displaced fear of my own masculinity. I did not want to grow up and become masculine because that meant being like my father—overpowering, cruel, and destructive.

A final example of how my heart symbolized my inner conflict is another dream. From early childhood until mid-adolescence, I had a recurring dream that never failed to awaken me in a sweaty panic. In the dream I am on one side of a huge green hedge, running from my father. He is on the other side, chasing me with a knife in his hand. When we come to the end of the hedge, I see him and I run away from him. As I am running, I see a closet door ahead of me. I open the door, go inside, and close the door behind me—only to find in front of me a dead man in a body bag. This dream represented symbolically what had happened to my masculinity. In fear, I was running away from my father (the masculine). The only place to go for refuge was in a closet where the masculine was dead. Only in the presence of the dead masculine did I feel safe.

When I split off from my masculinity, I invested more emotionally in my feminine qualities. But I came to hate the feminine in me. As a teenager looking at my pictures in the school yearbook, I always despised the feminine qualities I saw in myself. Because my masculinity was so repressed, the feminine in me was not rightly complemented with a masculinity appropriate for my biological sex, my maleness. Consequently, my feminine side emerged as a false femininity, an effeminacy.

Symbolic Confusion

As I grew up, my heart held no images of whole men. For that reason I could not recognize the masculine qualities that *were* in me. I had no standard by which to recognize the masculine and identify with it in a healthy way. In lieu of real symbols of masculinity, my heart provided me with false and unhealthy ones: the foot fetish, the fear of the overpowering maple tree, and the dream of my father chasing me. In the letter my sister Annelyse sent me along with the copy of *The Broken Image*, she wrote, "God is a perfect Father and longs to give His children good things." I remember reading those two words together—*perfect* and *father*—and saying to myself, "Perfect and father go together like fish and bicycle." My heart could not comprehend such an idea; it was an entirely abstract thought.

A child's encounters with disordered forms of masculine and feminine love register in his developing gender identity and in his understanding of gender complementation as confused symbols.

> When love is disordered, our relationships are disordered. Then primal images are missing or they are seriously (as in the homosexual neurosis) confused. This is the tragedy of broken homes where we sustain not only the loss of parents and other family members, but the loss of what these persons symbolize as well. We sustain the loss of symbolic images of wholeness that continue to nourish us.[3]

Love Story

Masculinity and femininity are communicated to us as children through those people in our lives who symbolize to us what masculinity and femininity are (initially mother and father). In order to acquire a healthy personal identity, we must encounter loving and healthy relationships with members of both sexes. It could be said that our early encounters with loved ones of both sexes register in our hearts as a story of love with specific ideas about masculinity and maleness and about femininity and femaleness.

Within the plot of this love story are storylines that shape our sense of identity. Our relationships to the characters in these storylines affect the direction our sexuality takes. If throughout development our relationships with members of both sexes are healthy, a healthy heterosexual story of love is written on our hearts. Our sexuality then follows that love story, and we live out those pleasant storylines of love between the sexes as written in our hearts.

For the development of a healthy sexual identity, the love story in the heart must contain two parallel storylines. One storyline is the love relationship with the same-sex parent. Within this storyline are good memories of bonding, with a joyful realization somewhere along the line that "this person is like me." The other storyline is the love relationship with the other-sex parent. Within this storyline are good memories of relating, with an early realization that "this person is other than me," that the differences between "me and this person are complementary and bring us closer together." Ideally, this complementarity between the sexes has been modeled to us by mother and father.

In order for us to identify with the same-sex parent and realize the complementary otherliness of the other-sex parent, our heart must contain positive images of both sexes in relation to each other. Failure to have healthy relationships with members of both sexes will imprint negative characters into the storylines of identification and complementation in the heart's love story. Our sexuality will then follow those storylines, and some form of gender and sexual ambivalence or confusion will ensue.

I use the term gender when referring to masculine qualities or feminine qualities as they exist in God and in humanity. As a term, it is often used to explain learned behaviors characteristically associated with biological maleness or femaleness. The term gender may also be used to refer to one's internal sense of belonging to one's own sex. One's "core gender identity" may be defined as a "biological self-image that results through the growth of one's own perception of self in relation to others."[4]

Gender, the qualities of masculinity and femininity, encompasses the sexes but is not limited to that which has a sex. As C. S. Lewis has written, "Gender is a reality and a more fundamental reality than sex."[5] Masculinity and femininity are qualities that exist in the Godhead. Because their origins are in God, masculinity and femininity can be seen as having transcendent dimensions. Dr. Donald Bloesch writes:

> While the biblical witness is clear that the living God transcends sexuality, that he is neither male nor female, it is equally clear that he encompasses masculinity and femininity within himself. Indeed, we are created in his image as male and female (Genesis 1:27; 5:1, 2).[6]

Moreover, in *Is the Bible Sexist?* Dr. Bloesch writes:

> [God] includes masculinity and femininity as movements within himself, indicating initiative and power on one hand (the masculine) and receptivity and loving obedience on the other hand (the feminine).[7]

God's primary relationship to us is that of masculine initiator (He loves first; He initiates redemption). Our primary relationship to God is that of feminine responder (receiving His love, receiving Christ into our hearts). God does act in feminine responsiveness toward human beings when we initiate contact with Him: "Come near to God and he will come near to you" (James 4:8). But our coming to Him is born out of His self-revelation to us that He is there to be contacted in the first place. Additionally, the Scripture uses feminine imagery to describe God's "motherly" love for humanity (i.e., Numbers 11:12 and Matthew 23:37). However, most of the language in the Scriptures describes God in masculine terms. God reveals Himself to the world as a Father in heaven, not a mother in heaven. As one theologian has said:

> The God of the Old Testament is not only designated as "Father," but declared to be *the* Father. Our Lord declared: "Call no man

your father on earth, for you have one Father, who is in heaven
(Matthew 23:9 RSV)."[8]

But fallen human beings have a distorted image of who God is
and of what it means to be made in His image—male and female
(Genesis 1:26). As fallen creatures, His image in us is over-
shadowed by sin, and as a result we live in confusion as to what
gender and sex are.

Masculinity and femininity are qualities that exist in every
human being. When Dr. Bloesch writes, "In their relationship to
God and Christ, all Christians are called to assume the role of the
feminine,"[9] or when C. S. Lewis states, "What is above and beyond
all things is so masculine that we are all feminine in relation to
it,"[10] what they are saying is that all of humanity, males and
females alike, are in the feminine position of responding to God's
acts of initiation (i.e., covenants, love, redemption). Moreover,
when we refer to the church as she (or as the Bride of Christ), we
do not mean that it is composed of females. Nor when we refer
to God as He (or to Christ as our Bridegroom) do we mean that
God is male.

Our Lord Jesus, being fully God and fully man, displays the
feminine quality of receptivity as He is always waiting and listening for the word the Father is sending. Jesus displays the masculine quality of initiation when, in obedience to the Father, He
freely lays down His life on the cross, providing redemption for
mankind.

It would be wrong, however, to so narrowly define the masculine as *only* the quality of initiation and the feminine as *only* the
quality of receptivity. That would be too simple, and we would
lose all the indescribable qualities contained within masculinity
and femininity. If defined too specifically, masculinity and femininity quickly degenerate to the stereotyped roles into which we
mistakenly try to fit men and women. The Hollywood depiction
of a mustached macho man or a bleached blonde airhead are
perfect examples of such caricatures. Here we lose the truth that
individual males and females are designed possessing both masculine and feminine qualities. Ideally, masculinity and femininity ought to coexist happily in the soul of every human being.

Yet many people mistakenly believe that only males have masculine qualities and that only females have feminine qualities. Consequently, women are categorized as primarily intuitive and men as primarily rational. A second misconception is that the only distinction between men and women is a biological one (sex), disregarding gender realities altogether. Those who hold to these two misconceptions confuse gender with sex. When they see the word masculine (gender), they read the word male (sex). They need to be reminded that masculine and feminine refer to gender-related qualities and that male and female refer to biological sex. Though one ought not to go too far in defining gender and sex apart from each other lest we fail to see them as interrelated, it is necessary to see the differences between these words. Andy Comiskey, in his book *Pursuing Sexual Wholeness*, writes:

> Maleness involves the state of being a man instead of a woman. It's directly related to one's biological gender. Masculinity is a quality, a posture, an approach to life that is complemented by femininity. Men and women alike will express both feminine and masculine qualities. . . . But to be whole men and women those qualities must find a harmony and a rhythm that is appropriate to their biological sex.[11]

Clearly, it is correct for a man to say that his is a masculine gender identity and for a woman to say that hers is a feminine one. We not only possess masculine and feminine qualities, but also by our sex we *belong* to one gender or the other. A secure sense of belonging to one's gender is central to having a healthy personal identity.

The extent to which we are in need of healing may reflect the degree to which we are in touch with our masculine and feminine qualities. If there is an imbalance between the masculine and the feminine, or alienation from one gender altogether, some form of dysfunction will appear in our personal identity. Leanne Payne, writing about this as it pertains to the need for healing, says:

> For a woman to be free to initiate—free, that is, to hear the word of the Lord and do what she hears Him say—is for her to be in

touch with her masculine side. She is not sickly passive—the feminine principle estranged from the masculine. She is free to respond to God with all her being, and therefore able to *initiate* when the occasion calls for it. In the upright, vertical relationship to her Lord, she is fully a person, fully enabled to collaborate with His Spirit. She is a balanced feminine *maker* in the image of her Creator Father.

Likewise, for a man to fully function as a masculine *maker*, he must be in touch with the feminine principle in him. His heart must be capable of *responding* to God, to others, to the work that is to be done. His heart, like that of his female counterpart's, is the fertile womb that continually receives the life of Christ and in response gives birth to the *making* God has ordained him to do. Listening obediently for the healing word that God is always sending, he becomes a servant and steward of that word, a nurturer of it in the hearts of others. He therefore becomes a healer of broken relationships. He is the masculine *bride* of God. Invariably when a soul needs healing, there will be an imbalance within of the masculine and feminine. He or she is tipping the scales too far toward one extreme of the continuum.[12]

For a better understanding of the development of a healthy heterosexual love story, consider three Greek words for love—storge, philia, and eros.

Storge

This term means something like "natural love" or "family love." It is the love that binds people in some natural group—the love of the family, for example. Parents love children and children love parents and children love one another. . . . Membership in a family meant a great deal to most people in antiquity, and storge accordingly was both a valuable and valued element in one's life. Without it, what was possible was nothing more than a miserable and deprived existence, something that could scarcely be called a life.

C. S. Lewis finds this form of love very important. He calls it "affection," and says of it: "The image we must start with is that of a mother nursing a baby, a bitch or a cat with a basket full of puppies or kittens—all in a squeaking, nuzzling heap together;

purrings, lickings, baby-talk, milk, warmth, the smell of young life."[13]

Storge love has masculine and feminine forms, and our encounters with these different forms of storge vary during childhood.

In infancy, we initially taste of storge in its feminine form via mother—a touch, a breast filled with nourishment. In the symbiotic relationship between child and mother, the infant is not even conscious that he is a separate being from mother. The infant only knows the feelings of security and love as a result of having been a part of her body.

> An invisible cord persists, long after the umbilical one is severed. There exists a deeply knowing relationship between child and mother—a mode of knowledge which precedes the advent of reason and, in a sense, transcends it.[14]

It is in the love of mother that an infant experiences a sense of being and selfhood. In her love, the infant's love story receives its first imprint of femaleness and femininity, and of being.

It is critically important that a child not be separated from the mother until he or she has developed the ability to understand her absence. Otherwise the infant internalizes her absence as rejection. Feminine love then connects with rejection as a theme in the heart's love story.

Psychologists who study the relationship between children and their parents generally agree that the ability to understand the mother's absence does not begin to develop until the ninth month of life and is not fully developed until about age two and a half. Long periods of separation from mother before this time cause not only feelings of rejection, but also a variety of negative effects—rage, anxiety, and even lust—in adulthood. (See Dr. Frank Lake's book *Clinical Theology* or Dr. John Bowlby's *Attachment and Loss*.)

In order to come into a secure sense of selfhood apart from mother, a child needs the loving affirmation of father. Dr. Daniel Trobisch has said, "Mother is a circle and father is the one who draws us away from that circle." The child's initial encounter with the masculine form of storge comes primarily as father loves mother; he loves the child through her. In his love for his wife, a father begins to write into his child's love story the theme of masculine care and nurturing. As children learn to crawl, they crawl away from mother to father. In his loving affirmation, he plays the important part of helping the child separate his or her personal identity from the mother's identity. As this pertains to development during adolescence Leanne Payne writes:

> Whether or not we accept ourselves as persons is dependent upon affirmation coming to us through the masculine voice. I cannot as a woman affirm my son or daughter in his or her gender identity. It is the male voice they are listening for, because as children of my womb, they are separating their identity from me. The bonds with the father before this crucial time of adolescence are of course important. Now, however, they are all-important. As the father comes "between" his sons and their mother where necessary, he enables them to separate their *sexual and personal identities* from hers. This is also true with the daughter, though not quite so crucial insofar as sexual identity is concerned. She is not, after all, *other* than mother.[15]

In the case of a son, the father's love will enable him to positively identify with the male and masculine characteristics he sees in his father. This is central to the development of a healthy "gender role identity"—the part one plays in life as a man or as a woman. To both his sons and daughters, father is a representation of all that is masculine and male in the world, just as to both her sons and daughters, mother is a representation of all that is feminine and female in the world. It is important that children positively identify with the gender roles they perceive in the same-sex parents in order to learn from them a positive gender role identity. Conversely, it is equally important for a child to positively experience gender differences with the other-sex parent in order to learn how to relate in a complementary fashion with members of the other sex. To be secure in our gender identity is to be properly identified with the same sex and to relate with a healthy complementarity toward the other sex.

One morning my sister Karen called me to share the latest cute thing my nephew Alexander had done. My brother-in-law had left for work that morning, and Karen went about washing the breakfast dishes. Her two children, Katie, five years old, and Alexander, two, went off into another room to play. Some time went by, and Karen failed to hear a peep from either of them, which she told me is usually a sign they are up to something.

Just as she was about to leave the kitchen and check on them, in walked Alexander, clumping along in his father's house shoes, wearing his father's glasses, and carrying his father's study Bible.

Karen then ran into the bathroom, thinking that Katie was also playing the same game. A few weeks earlier, Katie had covered her face with makeup and had taken scissors and chopped off a large section of her hair. Karen is a hair stylist by profession. This time, Karen found Katie happily playing in her own imaginary world with all hairs safely in place.

These innocent forms of play reveal a healthy symbolic iden- tification with the same-sex parent. The end product of healthy gender identification such as this is a healthy gender role iden- tity. This identification with one's gender is foundational for the establishment of healthy core gender identity, that is the deep- felt assurance a boy has that he is not only male but also that he is masculine, or of a girl that she is both female and feminine.

As this core gender identity grows, children awaken to the ways they differ from the other sex. Such an awakening not only affirms gender complementarity, but also more deeply affirms a child's growing identification with the same sex.

The mimicking of gender roles in play aids a child in securely identifying with the gender to which he or she belongs. In the 1920s Jean Piaget, a Swiss psychologist, did extensive study on the importance of childhood play.

> Piaget saw symbolic play as a very important aspect of a child's emotional life as well as of his or her cognitive development. . . . Play serves a multitude of functions. When you observe children

in play, you will learn a great deal about what they are trying to comprehend.[16]

Love from mother and father is the first imprint on the story-lines of gender identification and gender complementation in the love story of our hearts. The love a mother gives to her children is unique and different from the love a father gives to his children. It is important to appreciate these differences and not to value one love above the other. The loves given to us by mother and father are not interchangeable, but they are equally important. Security in parental love enables a healthy heterosexual love story to develop and later to be lived out. When healthy expressions of masculine and feminine storge have been imprinted into our hearts, we are free to have other forms of love written into our story.

Philia

As we begin our encounter with the world outside mother, crawling toward father, we eventually discover the world of friends.

A second word for love is philia, which means the love of friendship. It is the love of a man for his fellow, of a woman for her friend. This, too, points us to something of great value in life. It would be possible to live without friends, but it would be a very impoverished existence. Lewis points out that we do not seem to make as much of friendship these days as did the ancients, when Aristotle could classify it as one of the virtues and when Cicero could write a book about it.[17]

Friendship also has its feminine and masculine expressions. In early development, children seem not to notice whether their playmates are male or female. As the storyline of gender identification with the same sex develops in the love story of the heart, it is perfectly natural for a little boy, in discovering his "little-boyness," to want to play only with other boys. The same is true for little girls. When a child feels secure in his or her identification with the same-sex parent within the family, a need emerges to bond with members of the same sex outside the family circle. This is commonly called "troop-bonding," whereby membership in a group helps to further gender identification. A "yuk-girls" attitude in boys and a "yuk-boys" attitude in girls is perfectly natural during this period. This childish rejection of the other sex as not being "one of us" is part of healthy identification with the same sex. It is not healthy, however, to remain in this childish stage.

Play with the other sex is critically important in the development of a healthy storyline of gender complementation in the love story of the heart. Throughout childhood, and especially at puberty, friendship with the other sex should be encouraged by parents, teachers, and other significant authority figures. Otherwise the child's ability to relate to the other sex may be underdeveloped, repressed altogether, or in adulthood be tragically reduced to a sexually charged expression of eros.

Eros

In puberty eros emerges, usually at first immature, often sexually overcharged and dramatically colored with romanticism. Frequently it appears in our hearts like a tragic love story. If we are healthy at puberty, the storyline of gender complementation in the love story of the heart takes all the focus. For the young man in love, he becomes the central character in a subplot of erotic love. His feelings about the object of his love, his longing to have her, his thoughts about her become the main themes in this subplot. What is missing is equal attention to her feelings, her needs, and her thoughts. His motivation is characteristically narcissistic.

> . . . eros is what most people today have in mind when they think of love. Basically, eros is romantic love, sexual love. It is the name of the Greek god with the bow and arrows. *The word is used to refer to affections other than romantic love*, but this is its typical meaning, the one that gives it its particular character. We should note at the outset that eros is more than sexual experience. It is pos-

sible for the sex act to take place without love. . . . But the sex act is the fitting expression of eros. It is not itself eros, because affection is a primary element in this kind of love. (italics mine)[18]

Eros is the love between the sexes with all its differing expressions. It includes the complementary relating between a man and a woman, the innocent holding of hands of adolescents caught in puppy love, the simple pleasure a man receives in admiring a woman, and the truly intimate knowing and being known of the conjugal embrace. Healthy eros always includes mutual respect.

Eros is the appropriate term, not only for the love between the sexes that is expressed romantically, but also for the love relationships between the sexes within the family. The love a son has for his mother naturally includes aspects of eros simply because of their sexual difference. This is also true of the love a daughter has for her father.

Eros as expressed in romantic love desperately needs defining these days. Our society as a whole is like an adolescent who has failed to come out of puberty. The storyline of gender complementation in our hearts reads more like a tragic love story or a soap opera. We seem to be stuck in a narcissistic view of eros which is highly romanticized, or we fail to connect the sex act with love. Like helpless Romeos in search of our Juliets, we desperately need the profound insights C. S. Lewis gives in *The Four Loves:*

> Now Eros makes a man really want, not a woman, but one particular woman. In some mysterious but quite indisputable fashion the lover desires the Beloved herself, not the pleasure she can give.[19]

This other-directed description of love stands in stark contrast to the narcissistic self-gratifying lust that passes today for eros.

As a man, I am appropriately in touch with the difference between affection that I have toward a brother in Christ and affection I have toward a sister in Christ. The truest form of brother-to-brother love is philia as empowered by agape (God's unconditional love). Part of the love that I have for him is rooted in the fact that we are both males. In French, the word meaning to know as a result of similarity in birth is *connaitre*. *Naitre* means birth and *con* means the same.[20] This knowing by virtue of sameness can only come when the heart's storyline of identification with the same sex is healthy.

The truest form of love that I can have for a sister in Christ is also philia as empowered by agape, but it includes eros, simply because I am male and she female. Because I do not share the same nature with her (in her humanity yes, but not in her sex), I come to know her by experiencing her, by reaching out to her and bringing her into my embrace. In French this way of knowing is called *savoir*, from which we get our English word savor. This knowing by virtue of otherliness can only occur when the storyline of gender complementation in the heart is healthy.

Confused Love

"We love confusedly, we fallen ones; the journey of life is for setting love in order."[21] Our early encounters with the masculine and feminine forms of these three types of love, as embodied in our significant relationships (mother, father, and others), shape how we experience love toward the same sex and the other sex later in life. These encounters also affect how we view ourselves as men or women.

The storylines of gender identification and gender complementation cannot be written on the heart in isolation from each other. We can only truly know one by knowing the other. Masculine and feminine are defined as they are experienced in tandem. Consequently, if we are confused in one, we will be confused in the other.

Unmet love needs from childhood do not go away simply because we grow up. They often appear disguised as a neurotic need demanding to be met. If we are lacking in one of these different types of love, it is likely that we will try to meet that need in one of the other loves. The unmet love need turned neurotic may appear in the storylines of both gender identification and gender complementation.

When a man fails to receive the masculine form of storge during childhood, a deficit is written into his storyline of gender identification. He may try to fill that deficit by a clinging, dependent attachment to another male. Or he may try to fill it through an expression of eros, resulting in a homosexual neurosis. If the man has a deficit of philia, he may have unreasonable expectations of his male friends. The woman who has not come into a secure sense of being in mother's love may transfer this need into her relationships with other women, expecting from them what they simply cannot and ought not give. Some homosexuality, either in the male or the female, can be understood as unmet same-sex love needs that have become eroticized.

In these cases, eros has become mistakenly written into the storyline of gender identification, while at the same time it has been left out of the storyline of gender complementation. Because the needed love is storge, the attempt to receive that love in eros will never make up the deficit. One is literally "looking for love in all the wrong places." The unmet need for same-sex love becomes distorted and overblown. Some homosexuality, either in the male or in the female, results in a fearful avoidance of the other sex and a dependent attachment to the same sex. The introduction of eros into this storyline serves as a neurotic way of coming together and identifying with the same sex. By avoiding members of the other sex, the homosexual does not have to deal with his sense of sexual inadequacy in relation to them.

When the heart's love story is confused, so are our relationships with both sexes. In order to become healthy, we must honestly narrate our heart's love story to God and seek His insights as to how our hearts became so confused. In painful honesty, we can admit before God and others how broken relationships with loved ones have affected our identification with the same sex and complementation with the other sex. We can acknowledge how these broken relationships have shaped our personality. When we can look at the past in total honesty and see it as it truly was, then we can begin to come free from our reactions to the broken relationships that affect our relating in the present. Only then can we truly love and be loved by both sexes and thereby become the persons God intended us to be.

4

Setting Love in Order

Disengaging Symbolic Confusion

"Real isn't how you are made," said the Skin
Horse. "It's a thing that happens to you.
When a child loves you for a long, long time,
not just to play with, but REALLY loves you,
then you become REAL."
   "Does it hurt?" asked the Rabbit.
   "Sometimes," said the Skin Horse.[1]

                                    Margery Williams

Meeting a Whole Man

Our inner picture of who mother or father are will reflect their ability or inability to love us aright. Sometimes they tried to raise us never having known for themselves what it was to be loved rightly by their parents. All that mother and father literally are to us, as well as all that they represent to us, will be tainted if we experienced disordered love from them. Because mother and father are the prototypes of man and woman in our hearts, the way our hearts symbolize the sexes will reflect their brokenness.

When these all-important symbols are confused, they become the containers for misperceptions about masculine and feminine qualities within ourselves and others. Because these confused symbols reside within the unconscious, we are only aware of the emotions, attitudes, and behavioral patterns which spring forth from them into our consciousness. In adulthood, we simply come up with the wrong answer to the question, "What is a whole man like?" or "What is a whole woman like?"

During that momentous vacation I spent in Milwaukee taking Leanne Payne's class on personal wholeness, I met with someone on Leanne's ministry team—the associate pastor of the host church. Pastor Brown was a kindhearted man with a round, gentle face and the build of a wrestler. At our first meeting he asked me, "Mario, what is a whole man?"

Sitting there dumbfounded, I replied, "I don't know."

When I tried to visualize a whole man, my heart brought up a picture of my father ranting and raving in angry fits; of cruel schoolboys harassing me because I was effeminate; of men together in homosexual embraces—these were the only images my heart held of men.

He then asked me, "Do you remember any whole men from your childhood?"

"No." I couldn't think of one. The only inkling I had was from the stories my mother had told me about her father—how kind and gentle he always was and how he overflowed with love for his six daughters. But he too was a broken man, an alcoholic. Pastor Brown actually was the first whole man who ever took an interest in me.

Having a difficult time believing that I had gone through life never having met a whole man, he pressed the question, "Surely you met *one* whole man sometime in your life?"

Irritated, I snapped back, "Look, buddy, you probably grew up in some place like Indiana where as a boy you played Little League. And I'm sure your father came and rooted for you at your baseball games. Well, I didn't grow up like that. Now you will simply have to believe me that I have never in my entire twenty-five years on this planet *ever* met a whole man."

Lovingly, he looked me in the eye and did not react to my sarcastic reply. He took out his Bible and turned to Luke, chapter 7, the story of the centurion's faith. He explained to me how this man loved all people God put in his path, from his servant to the Jewish people in his area.

While the pastor explained to me this beautiful story with great love and care, I began to sense the love of a whole man—Pastor Brown. To me he was a real-life example of the good and loving centurion in the Biblical story. Every time he would look to his Bible to read another portion of the story, my eyes would sneak a look at his kind face, or at the gentleness of his hands, as if I were inspecting a creature from another planet. I had no idea how to relate to him.

At the end of our first session he took my hands into his, and we prayed together. It was the first time in my life that a whole man had reached out to me. When he took hold of my hands, I responded to his loving touch erotically, and I was too ashamed to tell him about my feelings. There was no place within my being to receive the agape-inspired masculine philia-love Pastor Brown was offering me. Additionally, eros had become written into my heart's storyline of gender identification. I knew only one way to interpret another man's loving touch—erotically.

While he was praying with my hands held so gently in his, I opened my eyes and peeked at his face. His sincerity increased the shame I was feeling for my body's erotic response. Then something Pastor Brown prayed caused me to receive a surge of real nonerotic love. I think it was when he referred to me as "my brother Mario" at the end of the prayer. Not only did I feel the love of God flow into me through this good man's hands, but I also felt real human love. His touch was more powerful than the neurotic feelings emerging from the symbolic confusion within me. Immediately, love began to be set in order.

His hands were tenderly solid and real compared to mine, which seemed like putty under his touch. As he prayed, I felt as if my hands were being molded. Indeed, I was being molded,

molded into the man Jesus died to redeem. This was painful, but I was becoming real.

Disengaging Diseased Mental Images

My true self began to emerge as the *real,* the *true,* and the *good* within Pastor Brown was mediated to me through his loving touch. Simply by being a faithful Christian, he became a sacramental channel through which God's healing flowed into me. What Pastor Brown was, a whole man in Christ, left a far deeper impression on me than what he said. My heart began to be resymbolized that day. The old distorted symbols of confused masculinity were disengaging from the storyline of gender identification in my deep heart. Now new images of whole masculinity began to find their rightful place there.

After leaving Pastor Brown's office, I felt for the first time that healing from homosexuality might be possible. I would not allow myself to actually hope for complete healing lest I be disappointed. I was only giving this healing stuff consideration because I felt God leading me in this direction, not because I had any great faith that it would work. Besides, I enjoyed the pleasure I experienced in homosexual encounters and did not know if I was ready to forsake this forever. However, I knew the healing I now thought possible could never happen without some moral effort on my part. Therefore, as long as I considered healing a possibility, I agreed before God not to engage in any homosexual activity.

Since having read Leanne Payne's book *The Broken Image* eight months earlier, I had begun praying again. The motivation behind much of my prayer was the desire to be free from all the negative feelings and memories I had of my father, not necessarily to be healed of homosexuality. Every morning in prayer, I asked Jesus to bring up from my heart just one memory where I could apply His divine forgiveness towards my very needy and unhealed father. Then I asked the Lord to forgive me for my sinful reactions to my father's sins against me. Every day for eight months, God showed me in prayer some memory that necessitated healing and forgiveness.

By the time I saw Pastor Brown, the cross of Jesus with its powerful ability to forgive sins in me and in others had greatly softened my stony heart. It was ready to be resymbolized. The old distorted images of men and women, and associated feelings and memories, were no longer cemented in my heart by bitterness and unforgiveness. But for the confused symbols to be replaced by real symbols, I had to face all the emotions, attitudes, and behaviors issuing from these confused symbols.

Inextricably linked to my homosexual neurosis was a homosexual fantasy life, often fed by pornography. As Leanne Payne points out, this kind of fantasy life, as well as the images that well up from the unhealed psyche, provide symbolic pictures of gender confusion to the individual.[2]

Turning from this fantasy life and the use of pornography was the first step to disengaging the diseased imagery of the sexes lodged in my mind. Additionally, I needed to repent of the lust behind these practices and receive healing for anxiety-driven masturbation. But these were practices I had engaged in daily for almost ten years. This was not going to be easy. After repenting of lust, I threw away every piece of pornography I owned.

Then I needed to deal with the diseased images in my mind. First, I looked for the meaning contained within the images in my homosexual fantasies. To use Leanne Payne's terminology, I needed to learn to read my "cannibal compulsion."

In *The Broken Image* Leanne tells the story of Matthew, a young man who, like myself, needed to disengage the symbolic confusion in his homosexual fantasies. When rightly understood, these symbols are confused cries from the heart for gender identification and personal integration with the same sex. Leanne begins her conversation with Matthew by asking him:

> "What do you do in your fantasies?"
>
> "In my fantasies I want to embrace him, to kiss him on the mouth. I want to come together with him. And in my dreams, that is what I do."
>
> After this reply I asked him, "Do you know anything at all about the habits of cannibals? Do you know why they eat people?"

In utter astonishment he replied, "No, I've no idea why they eat people."

This is a set of questions that are often key in bringing home to such minds and hearts as Matthew's what is really happening in homosexual compulsions. I then told him what a missionary once told me: "Cannibals eat only those they admire, and they eat them *to get their traits.*"

What was happening to Matthew was very clear; he was looking at the other young man and loving a lost part of himself, a part that he could not recognize and accept. (italics mine)[3]

Ruth Tiffany Barnhouse in her book *Homosexuality: A Symbolic Confusion* defines homosexuality as the neurotic attempt to gain gender identification with the same sex. She writes:

> . . . the homosexual adaptation may be resorted to in order to identify with the "masculine" strength of the partner. As one patient of mine expressed it, "It was not so much that I wanted to *love* Peter; I wanted to *be* Peter." (italics mine)[4]

Insight alighted in my mind and I firmly grasped this truth: My homosexual desire was not a biological drive, but was rather the projection of disordered love and incomplete gender identification onto a member of the same sex who symbolized my masculinity. I thus began putting to death the lie that homosexuality is a legitimate expression of human sexuality.

In order to disengage the confused symbols of masculinity within me, I asked myself these simple questions about the men who appeared in my sexual fantasies or about those toward whom I felt sexually attracted: What is it about this man that I am trying to take? What part of my masculinity does he symbolize that I am not in touch with?

It became apparent to me that all the men in my past whom I had been "in love" with were nothing more than the recipients of my projections. I was merely trying to complete my gender identification by erotic union with them. Actually, I had never seen them as the real flesh and blood persons they were, but had only related to them from the perspective (even if unconscious) of my own neediness and confusion.

Freedom from Anxiety-Driven Masturbation

Following my increasing release from diseased mental images, I knew I had to begin dealing with the ingrained habit of masturbation and related anxiety. Because masturbation is often driven by anxiety, I do not think it wise to speak of one without the other. However, for the sake of clarity in writing I will discuss them separately.

Always masturbating in the same place, my bedroom, and right before I went to sleep at night, I had come to associate my bedroom with this behavior. Every time I walked into my bedroom, I'd have a Pavlovian reflex, and I'd think about masturbating. My bedroom needed to be resymbolized—that is, in my heart it needed new meaning.

First, every time I felt the urge to masturbate, I simply got out of bed and knelt on the floor. Then I prayed the Lord's words to St. Paul about his weakness, "My grace is sufficient for you, for my power is made perfect in weakness" (2 Corinthians 12:9), until the urge subsided. Admitting my weakness before God, I asked for His strength to be poured into me. Never did I deny that the urge was there; I merely began to exercise some authority over my own body. Then I would return to bed and attempt to fall asleep again.

The first night I tried this, I got in and out of bed to pray ten or twelve times. I got very little sleep. However, by the time morning came, I had not masturbated. This was the first time in years that a twenty-four-hour period had gone by without my engaging in that behavior.

Still influenced greatly by beliefs about sexuality that I had picked up in the gay lifestyle, this seemed very unnatural to me. In my prayer journal I wrote:

> I did not masturbate last night; it seems so unnatural to not engage in so natural a behavior. But my perception about what is and what is not natural is no longer the standard in my life—Jesus is. I will do what I hear Him telling me to do, over what I think.

No longer were my egoistic subjective feelings and thoughts the measure of truth. Jesus was now my standard of truth. It was a strange paradox, having two contradictory sets of beliefs that I was personally committed to—one coming from my own un-healed heart and the other coming from my faith in God.

The next night the same struggle ensued, but I did not yield to the urge. The third night I did yield, but I knew better than to be unforgiving toward myself. I simply began again the next night.

Soon my bedroom was resymbolized. It became a place of communion with God and of rest. No longer was it associated in my heart with masturbation.

Infantile Separation Anxiety

At age two I was hospitalized for over a month with an upper respiratory infection. During this month, my mother was not per-mitted to be in the same room with me. In prolonged isolation from her, I developed severe separation anxiety. As a child, I car-ried this anxiety and the related defenses of shame, rage, and rejection deep within me. At puberty I began experiencing a dread-ridden urge to masturbate as a means to ease this anxiety. As I progressed into adulthood, masturbation became a habit-ual response to ease all tension and anxiety. In hindsight, I can see that while I was in the homosexual lifestyle, stressful situa-tions often sent me into a cycle of sexual activity.

In infancy children do not know they are separate individuals from their mothers. To be separated from the mother's physical presence is to be separated from their source of being. Children come into their own sense of being and into a sense of well-being through proper attachment to their mothers. To achieve this is to know a deep inner peace in mother's love. Infants are deeply aware of mother as their source of life. This intense awareness cannot be confused with or equated with biological drives such as the need for food. It goes deeper and is more elementary. As a result, children try constantly to maintain close proximity to mother.

When my nephew Alexander was just a few weeks old, I observed his need to stay close to my sister Karen. She and I were in the kitchen talking while she prepared dinner. Alexander was seated upright in his baby seat on the kitchen table observing his mother with his big blue eyes. Wherever she moved, his eyes followed her like a spotlight illuminating an actor on a stage. At one point, Karen left the kitchen. The moment Alexander lost eye contact with his mother, he began to fuss and eventually cried. But as soon as Karen reentered and he once again made eye contact with her, his tears came to a sudden end.

Though separation from mother is inevitable if a child is to mature into a healthy individual, the timing of such separation should coincide with a key stage of development during infancy. Commenting on a child's ability to positively experience separation, Dr. Sally Provence writes:

> A child's ability to cope with the stress of separation depends significantly on the capacity to evoke the mental images of those to whom they attribute their sense of security and well-being.[5]

This ability to evoke mental images is called evocative memory. A child has developed evocative memory when he or she learns that an object continues to exist when it is no longer in sight. If the child can reconstruct in the imagination a picture of mother and thereby know that she continues to exist when out of sight, he or she will not suffer severely from separation anxiety. My nephew Alexander could not mentally evoke a picture of his mother, nor could he understand that she was simply out of sight but still in the same house with him. When she left the room, he began to cry. All he knew was that she was gone.

Dr. John Bowlby, well-known attachment theorist, warns that prolonged separation from mother during the child's first three years of life is "dangerous and whenever possible should be avoided."[6] Dr. Bowlby observed three stages in the response of children to separation. The first stage is protest. In this stage the child screams and cries and looks for mother. All children experience this stage of separation anxiety insofar as all children at one time or another cry for their mothers when they are absent. The second stage is despair. During this stage the child loses hope for mother's return and withdraws into himself. The third stage is detachment. At this point the child regains interest in his environment and does not respond positively to mother when she returns. Only children who experience prolonged separation from mother enter into the last two stages of separation anxiety.

Dr. Frank Lake in his book *Clinical Theology* noted that separation anxiety may cause a variety of defenses and reactions in infants—rage, lust, genital tension, or rejection. Prolonged separation from mother may physically manifest in a child as painful genital tension. The child then grabs at the genitals to soothe the tension, much as an athlete rubs a sore muscle to ease its pain. Dr. David Benner adds that in a prolonged separation from mother, a child often feels shame resulting from a sense of worthlessness.[7] The child felt that he or she was not wanted.

Infantile reactions such as rage, lust, genital tension, rejection, and shame may persist into childhood, adolescence, and adulthood. In such cases, the child's behavior of rubbing the genitals to alleviate painful genital tension is sometimes misinterpreted by parents as masturbation. However, once the child enters adolescence, the rubbing of the genitals naturally results in sexual stimulation in the form of masturbation. But, as Leanne Payne has said, "in these cases, a dread-ridden masturbation (rather than a merely lustful one) ensues."[8]

The insight that some of my sexual urges related directly to anxiety, and not completely to homosexual lust, was freeing. As I progressed in my healing from homosexuality, I began to deal with the pain of infantile separation anxiety. Prayer with the laying on of hands played a major part in my healing. Such prayers always included a petition to God for me to receive a sense of well-being. An example of this kind of prayer follows:

> Dear Heavenly Father, I confess to You the sin of a fallen world where infants are born without a sense of relatedness to mother and without a sense of peace in her love. If, Lord, my relationship to my mother was disrupted by sin on her part, I do forgive her now for her sin. If, Lord, this was due to some other circumstance of this fallen world, I do forgive the sinful circumstance.

For whatever reason, Lord, I lost or never made a secure attachment to my mother. I have felt at times as if I had no being, as if I were falling through the cracks of life, related to no one and desperately alone. Enter into my lack of a sense of being and fill me, Lord, with the love I need in order to be related to others.

Lord, there is no peace within me—only gnawing anxiety that seems to grow worse when I am alone. Enter into my aloneness so that I may face it before You. Fill my emptiness with Your love. Gather up my loneliness and transform it into a garden of solitude.

Enter into my anxiety, Lord. Let Your peace enter into my pelvis where this anxiety has manifested as genital tension. Fill me with Your peace and, in doing so, heal the anxiety I've tried to alleviate through neurotic sexual behavior. I pray this in Jesus' holy name. Amen.

The Woman in New York

For women with the lesbian neurosis, the dread of being disrelated to the mother is often a root to their sexual problems. The lesbians' detachment from their source of being has not only caused intense anxiety, but also alienation from their primary relationship and, therefore, their means for acquiring a healthy gender identity. From early on in childhood, as a result of this anxiety, they may be carrying anxious tension in their genitals. Their need for feminine storge love may be so confused that all relationships with women may have become eroticized.

In counseling, such women will often tell me that the skin of their arms aches to touch and to be touched. This is a result of tactile deprivation. However, any touch from women is often confusedly received as erotic (as I responded to Pastor Brown's touch). As a result, they may not let anyone come too close for fear of eroticizing even the most simple forms of affection.

At a large conference outside New York City where I was teaching, I ministered along with a female minister to a lesbian woman with such needs. As we began praying for this distraught woman, I received a picture from the Lord. It was a toilet bowl. After telling this woman about what I was seeing, I asked her, "Does this have any significance to you?"

In great shame she began to weep and told us the horrible memory of a situation when she was five years old. Her mother found her sitting on the toilet as she was anxiously rubbing her genitals. Looking at her in disgust, her mother accused her of masturbating, thus inflicting on this already hurting child great shame and guilt.

We immediately dealt with the false shame and guilt she had been carrying for over forty years. We anointed her with holy water, symbolically communicating to her the cleansing of all her sins by Christ and putting to flight any oppressing spirits of shame and guilt. Then I assured her, "It is unusual for five-year-old little girls to masturbate. But some may rub their genitals to ease painful tension which has centralized there. This may be the tension of severe dread and anxiety resulting from not being rightly attached to mother."

After invoking the presence of Christ into this memory, we applied the forgiveness of Jesus to this broken mother-daughter relationship. It was then necessary to pray for the healing of the wounding effects from that broken relationship. I anointed her with oil. While I asked God to set into her a secure sense of being in mother's love, Willa, the woman who was ministering with me, tightly held this hurting woman in her arms. We waited and watched as God did just that.

Asking God to bless the feminine in this woman, I prayed that she would be able to properly receive the loving touch of Willa's embrace. She then told us that there was an impulse in her to eroticize Willa's touch. We asked God to enter into that impulse, to dispel any shame or guilt, and to set love in order. We then asked God to let His loving presence enter into all the muscles of this woman's body and to release any tension which had centralized in her feminine organs. It is not uncommon for women with severe separation anxiety to also experience unusually excruciating pain when menstruating. This is because the pain of separation anxiety compounds the existing pain of their menstrual cycle.

When we saw her the next morning, her face radiated joy and peace. She was a faithful Christian, and although this was but one of many healings God had done in her life, it was perhaps the greatest aside from her conversion. She would still have to walk this healing out and, as in her case, would be tempted by Satan to minimize it and would have foolish Christians negate it. But she had the Christian maturity to look up and out of herself and to keep her focus on Jesus.

It is preferable to have a woman hold the one in need when praying this type of prayer because it is the feminine form of storge love they lack. However, when a woman is not available, a man with a proper understanding of therapeutic touch can be used by God to pray for such a healing for men and women alike.

A Related Anxiety-Induced Behavior

Recently I have met persons struggling with another form of anxiety-driven masturbation, that of anal stimulation. There may be serious shame and guilt surrounding this problem. Once again, these feelings must be dispelled with great love and grace in order to properly deal with the problem.

These sufferers almost always are carrying serious tension in the sphincter muscles within their rectum. It is related to the tension they have carried in the lower parts of their body. They are always amazed when they find they can release this muscle tension simply by sending a message into that part of the body to relax.

If there is any lust associated with this behavior, it must first be repented of and put to flight. In almost all of these instances, it is necessary to pray for a sense of being or well-being to be set in.

Sexual Arousal and Anxiety

Clinical psychologists have long understood that anxiety-provoking situations often arouse a person sexually. One researcher noted a young man who "described how since his early teens he would get slight erections whenever he was feeling anxious."[9] The remedy for this anxiety-induced sexual arousal is to learn some practical skills in dealing with the anxiety, and not focus on the masturbation that occasionally results from it. Once the anxiety level is reduced, the masturbation urge will also subside.

In my own case, after receiving a secure sense of well-being, I continued responding to some anxiety with the urge to masturbate. I did not allow any false guilt to enter in at this time. It would only have escalated my anxiety level, which in turn would have increased the urge to masturbate. However, these temptations were very different from the lust-filled ones I experienced while still a homosexual or from the legitimate sexual need I now feel for union with woman as a normal young unmarried man.

For the man in transition out of homosexuality and into heterosexuality, some urges to masturbate come from the emergence of his repressed heterosexuality. His may be a belated experience of the sexual awakening toward woman that occurs normally during puberty. This awakening not only needs to be welcomed, but also called into maturity. And the individual must learn that simply because he has a legitimate sexual need, he does not have license to immediately meet it.

Sexual temptation related to anxiety became especially apparent to me after several visits to my parents' home—still the same tension-filled, dysfunctional home of my youth. During and after these visits I battled the temptation to masturbate. Learning some practical skills to deal with stress helped me to break this pattern. First, I established healthy boundaries between myself and the people in my family who caused the most anxiety. Second, I learned the survival skill of detachment, a must for any person who grew up in a dysfunctional family. "Detachment is releasing or detaching from a person or problem *in love.* We mentally, emotionally, and sometimes physically disengage ourselves from unhealthy (and frequently painful) entanglements with another person's life and responsibilities, and from problems we can't solve. . . . Detachment does not mean we don't care. It means we learn to love, care, and be involved without going crazy."[10] Finally, I limited my visits to my childhood home to only a few days at a time.

Prayer became the most important tool in dealing with this anxiety and related sexual arousal. First, I called on the name of Jesus and entered into dialogue with Him about what was happening. Then, speaking kindly to my body in the prayer, I'd say, "That's OK, body, you just go right ahead and feel anxious. Jesus is here, and He will calm you down. (While feeling both the anxiety and the sexual arousal, I continued praying.) Jesus, please enter into these two feelings and begin to separate the link my body has made between anxiety and sexual feelings."

This is a prayer I've had to pray often for myself. The goal of the prayer is not to stop the body from having sexual feelings. The goal is that sexual feelings will not be the result of anxiety. Sometimes I prayed, "Lord, let sexual feelings occur in my body only as a result of the proper relationship between myself and a woman."

Fasting and Prayer

One final word, something that helped me overcome masturbation and progress in my healing was the Christian practice of fasting. When the Christian fasts, he is telling his body, "I have authority over you. I am not a slave to my every fleshly desire." Just as the toddler learns control over his bowels during potty training, so too adults must learn self-control over urges within their members.

Coming from a background where I not only acted on every physical urge, but neurotically indulged in it, I found fasting to be a dynamic healing discipline for my Christian walk. When confronted with an issue I could not seem to get victory over, I often made it the object of my prayers while fasting. Frequently during these times of prayer and fasting, the Lord would speak some insight to me that advanced my healing.

As my need for deep emotional healing lessened, these times of fasting and prayer have become wonderful experiences of communion with God and especially sensitive times of prayer for discerning His will.

Disengaging Cruising

While new in the gay lifestyle in New York City, I remember looking at everyone on the streets with a sense of awe. I had grown up in the Midwest, and New York City was like the land of Oz to me. I quickly noticed that some men looked back at me in an unusual way. When a homosexual friend and I walked on Fifth Avenue, it happened again. So I asked him what these weird looks meant.

He said, "Oh, they're cruising you."

"What does that mean?" I asked.

"While you walk down the street, if you see a guy in the distance you might like and he looks back at you as if he might be interested, as you approach each other on the sidewalk, you check out each other. After you've both passed by, look over your shoulder, and if you're *both* looking back at each other, that means it's OK to make contact. Then there's the possibility that something might happen. It's called cruising."

For years I had been looking at men with the hope that they would look back at me as if they wanted me. Cruising is the confused way the homosexual sufferer tries to get a masculine look that says, "I want you," "I love you," "I need you." Cruising is but one expression of symbolic confusion.

As I was being healed of my homosexual neurosis, I came across an article in the Sunday *New York Times Magazine.* The article by David Shorewood quotes a letter from his brother Andy, an aging homosexual living in Paris.

> "I turn many fewer heads than I used to," he now writes. "A friend and I have a pastime we call 'Existing,' which consists of guessing if a stranger is aware of us, and if so, of which one, or whether we obviously don't 'exist' and are looked through, not at."
>
> These strangers, by whom Andy and his friends define their "existence," are boys and men first seen from afar, then from up close as they pass one another on the sidewalk.
>
> "When we do get a glance," he adds, "it is usually for Patrice, who is 15 years younger."
>
> Andy can handle the increasing absence of glances from strangers. But he is encumbered by having never seduced an affectionate glance from our father.[12]

My own father's looks at me never expressed love or affirmation; often they were filled with cruel mocking. One of my father's employees once said to me, "Mario, your father is the only man I know who can castrate another man with a dirty look."

Affirmation from one's father comes not only by what he says, or doesn't say, but also by his touch and his gaze. In not having received the needed affirmation—a positive assertion about our being, our existence—our hearts become confused. As a result, we seek to take that affirmation and love symbolically in an inappropriate manner.

Long after masturbation and overt homosexual temptation ceased to be a problem, I found myself still cruising. One night while driving home from a lay counseling course I was taking, I noticed that every time I'd pass a car, I'd look into it hoping I would see a man driving. I asked the Lord why. Although I did not hear a response, I knew better than to judge myself without mercy.

Shortly afterward, I was having dinner with a friend who had overcome homosexuality, and I asked him about it. He said, "I don't know why I did it, but I know how to pray about it. Every time I see a man that I am tempted by, I close my eyes, and I imagine the woman that God created for him to be with. As I see them together, I thank God that this man was created to become one flesh with his intended mate, which is a woman and not me."

Taking my friend's advice, I began telling my deep heart the truth. Every time I'd pray in this way, I would drop the image of man and woman together into my heart. In practice, God was resymbolizing my heart as he removed from it the old distorted images of men wrongly together with men and replaced them with whole and true images of men and women rightly related to each other. This process advanced greatly as I integrated into the body of Christ and there witnessed beautiful and whole marriages, men and women together, male and female in the image of God.

Sinful Responses to Loneliness

Dr. Frank Lake in his book *Clinical Theology* writes:

Patterns of loneliness in the present tend always to invoke their prototypes lying dormant at the roots of being. Working this way, the buried past turns a tolerably fearful present moment into an intolerably anxious one.[11]

He then goes on to say that "present loneliness can induce neurotic anxiety," which may in turn elicit from the sufferer sexual feelings leading to temptation.

For some, even though they have received a sense of being or well-being through prayer, they may continue to have sinful responses to loneliness—a loneliness which in the past occasionally resulted in sexual falls to alleviate the neurotic anxiety. Some of these sinful responses to loneliness are passivity (sloth), selfishness, and pride. I was guilty of all three.

The passive response is directly related to the self-pitying voice of the unhealed inner child. It is unimaginative and does not even bother to think of alternatives to this passive state.

While caught in this passive state, often lying on my couch and staring aimlessly into space, I'd sometimes bemoan my sad state to God in what I thought was a prayer. (Actually I was practicing the presence of the old Mario.) Once, when I sighed out one of these feeble prayers, the Lord answered by quickening Job 38:2–3 to my heart. Imagine my surprise when I looked it up and read: "Who is this that darkens my counsel with words without knowledge? Brace yourself like a man; I will question you, and you shall answer me."

I then read the following two chapters of Job aloud as I stood upright before God in my living room. The questions the Lord put before Job are so awe-inspiring that I could not read them without looking up and out of myself and receiving some perspective on my situation. After repenting of my passivity, I left that prayer more a man than when I entered it.

The selfish response to loneliness often comes from guarding one's privacy and not letting anyone in. It may be related to years of being alone and results in the individual forsaking fellowship with other Christians.

One Sunday morning when I had been out of the gay lifestyle for a little less than a year, the Lord convicted me of my selfishness. At the coffee hour after our church service, one of the leaders invited me to her home for a newcomers' brunch. "No thank you," I said kindly. "I have other plans." My "other plans" were nothing more than to spend the afternoon at the best Jewish deli in town, leisurely reading the *New York Times,* eating a bagel with lox and cream cheese, and sipping hot coffee. This had been a ritual in my life for five years.

As I drove to the deli, the Lord convicted me that I failed to consider her feelings or the love with which she had labored to prepare that brunch. The closer I got to the deli, the worse I felt. The *New York Times* would wait for me, but this brunch was happening only today. Finally, I turned the car around and went to the brunch where I met many people and later had more fellowship with them.

The prideful response may express itself as an unrealistic standard when picking friends. Rather than receiving all God's people as He brings them to us for fellowship, we may have a measuring stick by which we decide who is worthy of our time. Or relating to persons we deem to be better than ourselves may be a way of boosting low self-esteem. On the one hand we see ourselves as less than others and want their acceptance to feel better about ourselves. On the other hand we esteem ourselves higher than others and don't want to be bothered.

Even though I was from the Midwest and had received powerful ministry from that little church in Ohio, I occasionally found myself looking down my acquired long, cosmopolitan nose at these "farm people." Dayton, Ohio, was an insult to my (acquired) cultured Boston aesthetic sense. I felt I had done them a favor by coming to Cow-hio (that's what my friends in Boston called Ohio).

However, I felt great shame (true moral shame) once I recognized my arrogance. After all, it was equally hard for these people to reach to me across the cultural barriers between us. Still they looked past all my attitudes and fashionable New York East Village clothing and managed to love me.

We can deal with all these sinful responses to loneliness by properly repenting of them before God. If we don't, our loneliness will only continue and may lead to anxiety, which in turn may subject us to unnecessary temptation.

Facing Anxiety before God

After receiving so much help from Pastor Brown, from Leanne's class, and from repenting and being filled with the Holy Spirit, I had a most incredible experience with God one weekend. It was Thursday afternoon, and classes were canceled for Friday. Three long nights and two empty days awaited me before Sunday morning came and fellowship with other Christians. Sitting in my comfortable little apartment in Ohio, I began to feel the dread of being alone for such a long time. The sexual arousal linked to this anxiety resulted in overwhelming homosexual temptations. I knew full well that if I left my apartment, I would surely have a sexual fall.

Deciding to stay at home that evening, I watched a little television and did some reading. When Friday morning came, again deep anxiety and overwhelming homosexual temptation gripped me the moment I awakened. Except now these feelings seemed to have grown worse over the night. That morning during my devotions, I heard God say to me, "I love you, Mario." At the end of that prayer session a deep God-given assurance filled me: If I could make it through until Sunday morning without a sexual fall, then never again would my body be devoured with homosexual temptation like this. I just knew it. Aligning my will with God's will and deciding that a sexual fall was out of the question, I took out a Band-Aid and placed it over the inside of my front door and the molding around it. Then I promised God I would not break that seal until Sunday morning came, no matter how anxious or sexually tempted I became.

As Friday afternoon and evening progressed, the temptation and anxiety grew worse—something I did not think possible. I cleaned every corner of my apartment, straightened files I hadn't looked at in years, wrote letters to old friends, made long-distance phone calls and, above all, practiced the presence of Jesus. Friday night was spent primarily tossing and turning in what seemed like the longest night of my life. The Band-Aid seal was still on the door.

Saturday morning came. Now I faced a spotless apartment, orderly files, and a stack of letters written to people I hadn't corresponded with in years. All I could do was pray, read, and practice the presence of Jesus. Inside me the gnawing anxiety and forceful homosexual temptation still raged.

That afternoon, all alone in my living room, I read aloud and performed a one-person play, *The Passion of Lady Bright,* by Joe Orton, a gay playwright. The play tells the story of an aging male homosexual who is no longer young enough to attract bedfellows. His walls are covered with the signatures of all the one-night stands he has brought home over the past twenty years. As the play unfolds, he tries to remember the faces attached to the hundreds of signatures that adorn his walls. Some he remembers; while others he cannot. It is a sad play, but a truthful one, as in the end he realizes he is an aging homosexual with no one to love. In the play, Lady Bright is really a burned-out old queen living in a monologue, utterly alone and without hope.

After finishing my living room performance of this play, I fell to my knees in horror. Crying out to God, I begged, "Dear Lord, please don't let me become another Lady Bright." At that point, I remembered one of my most frightful memories from the gay lifestyle.

It was Christmas Eve, four years earlier. Several friends and I went out for a drink to one of our favorite gay bars. The city was covered with a layer of freshly fallen snow, and large flakes quietly and slowly dropped from the sky. As we walked from our car to the bar, a church bell struck midnight.

"Hey, it's Christmas morning," one of my friends said. "Merry Christmas."

Just as we approached the front door of the bar, it swung open and out stumbled a drunken older homosexual man. He fell on the snow-covered sidewalk, let out a profane expletive, managed to return to an upright position, and then staggered past us. The same friend who had wished us all a Merry Christmas contemptuously sneered, "How would you like to be that old fag on Christmas morning?"

As he said this, a shocking stillness came over me. With piercing sincerity I spoke out the thought I knew we all feared. "In thirty years, I am going to *be* that lonely old fag on Christmas morning." Without a doubt, if we continued as we were, we would all one day become Lady Brights or old trolls hiding in the shadows of gay bars. What we become when we live our lives apart from God is horrible.

Although I now struggled with homosexuality, I was not alone. I was not living in the arid monologue described in Orton's play. There but for the grace of God went I. I had entered into a living dialogue with God. I thought to myself, *Better to be suffering before the cross than to end up alone and hopeless.* The words of Job 13:15 rang in my ears, "Though he slay me, yet will I hope in him." Even if my present temptations never let up, I would stand before the cross and hurt, till kingdom come if necessary. Unable to form any words to pray, my painful, anxious loneliness became my prayer. There, in the midst of unbearable suffering, I resolutely decided to obey God. That is exactly what God was waiting for me to do.

Although my will was still feeble and in need of much more healing, I had exercised it in concert with God's will. God's presence abiding with me empowered me to do what I had previously thought impossible. With Christ, I faced the fear of loneliness, anxiety, sexual temptation, and abandonment I never before could face. This was a turning point in my healing as I voluntarily died to my old self and identified with Christ in His suffering. When Sunday morning came and I broke the Band-Aid seal on my door, my true self, the self in union with the resurrected Christ, was more firmly established as the center of my soul.

The next week I came into a powerful new realization of Christ living in me. It has changed my life. And never again did I have to face a gut-wrenching three-day weekend like that.

5

Christin Us

The Hope of Glory

> I have made you known to them, and will con-
> tinue to make you known in order that the love
> you have for me may be in them and that I
> myself may be in them. (Jesus speaking to the
> Father about you and me)
>
> John 17:26

Incarnational Reality

The power of the great truth, "Christ in you, the hope of glory" (Colossians 1:27), became a tangible reality in me a few months after I received that life-changing infilling of the Holy Spirit. I was by this time in the habit of beginning every day by setting my eyes on God through Scripture reading and prayer.

After reading Brother Lawrence's *The Practice of the Presence of God* and accounts of Frank C. Laubach's spiritual walk, I decided to start trying some of the things they did. I would call to mind the holy name of Jesus as often as possible. First, I decided to call on His name at least once each hour of the day. Gradually I would increase to once every half hour, then to every fifteen minutes, then to calling on Him every minute. Of course I failed miserably at the beginning, sometimes with hours going by without thinking of it. Then I would simply begin again, making sure not to inflict any false guilt on myself for not doing it. After a while, I found if I forgot to practice God's presence, I would be reminded by the Spirit within me to do so. On many a morning I would awake and hear the Spirit calling on the name of Jesus from within me. Soon I noticed that whenever my thoughts would wander, they would wander toward Him.

As I purposefully practiced the presence of God by looking up and out of myself and calling to mind the name of Jesus as often as possible, I began to notice the beauty of the world around me—in my students, my cat, the landscape of southeastern Ohio.

One spring afternoon, I sat in the office of the Chairman of the Theater Department at the university where I was teaching. The rest of the faculty filled the chairs around the chairman's desk. Behind his desk was a large picture window with the drapes fully opened. The winter's snow had melted, and green leaf buds dotted every tree branch.

Shortly after the meeting started, my thoughts began to wander. I began to give thanks to Jesus for the beauty of His creation and for the budding trees outside the window.

Noticing that my full attention was not invested in the meeting, the chairman asked me, "Mario, are you with us?"

"Sorry," I replied.

As the meeting continued, I was extra careful not to gaze out this large picture window. Rather, at the next moment of boredom, I looked down at my hands and gently pinched the skin over one of the knuckles of my left hand with the thumb and index finger of my right hand. While lifting this tiny pinch of skin off my knuckle and suspending it between my two fingers, I thought to myself, *God's beauty and reality is being mediated to me through the spring scene outside the window; how much more beautiful and real is the Spirit of God indwelling this tiny pinch of my skin.*

Suddenly the meaning of Christ being *in* me washed over me like waves of living waters. I then realized that if God's Spirit was mysteriously living in that tiny pinch of skin being lifted off my knuckle, that His very presence was also permeating through every cell and fiber of my body, whether I felt it or not. The words of 1 Corinthians 6:19–20 (RSV) flowed through me like life-giving blood: "Do you not know that your body is a temple of the Holy Spirit *within* you, which you have from God? You are not your own; you were bought with a price. So glorify God in your body."

While this truth was still flowing through my mind, I looked at the tip of my pinky finger and realized that if all I had of the Spirit of God indwelling me was what was in the tip of this tiny finger, I would have enough divine power to be healed. From that moment forward, I knew in the deepest part of my heart that I would be completely healed from homosexuality. And I eventually was. Sheer joy welled up from within me. I must have been glowing with religious awe.

Unknown to me, the chairman had been catching glimpses of me during this entire time. As I stared in wonderment at the tip of my pinky and the reality of the power of God indwelling it, he asked in a most peculiar voice, "Mario, what on earth is going on over there?"

Embarrassed that I had once again been caught not paying attention, I replied, "Oh, you'd never understand this if I told you."

"Try me," he quipped.

Not knowing any other words to use to describe my discovery of this age-old truth, I joyfully shared with him and the rest of the faculty members a term I had learned from Leanne Payne. "I've just come into Incarnational Reality!"

His face went completely blank, and he stared at me without any expression for several seconds. Then his eyes blinked a few times, and he finally looked away without saying a word back to me. The faculty meeting simply continued.

From that day forward, I related to my body in a completely different way. It wasn't just a body; it was the temple of the Holy

Spirit. Whenever I had a sinful fleshly desire, I refused to despise my body for it. Rather, I practiced the presence of the Holy Spirit *indwelling* me and focused on Jesus until the sinful desire and temptation ceased. This is not some pie-in-the-sky platitude nor esoteric theology. It is a down-to-earth, practical and ordinary reality available to every Christian.

Union with Christ

When I first came to Christ in my teens, I never heard any teaching on union with Christ through the Holy Spirit indwelling the believer. It was only ten years later, after attending Leanne Payne's adult Christian education class and later receiving the powerful infilling of the Holy Spirit at that little church in Ohio, that I came into the reality of "Another living in me." This reality is a central truth to the healing of persons.

In every Christian there is *a healthy place within,* that internal place where he is in union with Christ. About those who love Him, Jesus said, "My father will love him, and we will come to him and make our home with him" (John 14:23b). From that home within, we can dare to listen to our hearts and all that is within them. The Christian who finds after conversion that his heart is filled with garbage (as I did) is equipped to sort through all his inner confusion once he is assured of that healthy place within, that place where Jesus and the Father have made their home.

Of the eighty times the word union appears in Today's English Version of the New Testament, seventy-nine times it refers to the believer's union with Christ. One seminary professor of mine constantly reminds his students, "The theme of being 'in Christ' is so prevalent in the writings of St. Paul that it practically appears on every page of his epistles."

This mystical union between the believer and God is the reality that empowers us to be transformed from the inside out. It ought not to be confused with monism where God is in everything, or with New Age (gnostic) notions about man being or becoming God. As Orthodox theologian Father Kallistos Ware has said, "Although 'oned' with the divine, man still remains man; he is not swallowed up or annihilated. . . ."[1]

This union with Christ also empowers the believer's prayer life. Evangelical theologian Dr. Donald Bloesch writes:

> Still another way in which Christ makes a genuine prayer life possible is by his dwelling within the hearts of believers. He not only intercedes for us in heaven, but by his Spirit he makes his abode within the deepest recesses of our being. We can therefore call on him with confidence and assurance because he is infinitely near. Paul reminds his hearers, "Do you not realize that Jesus Christ is in you?" (2 Corinthians 13:5) Confidently he proclaimed, "Christ in you, the hope of glory" (Colossians 1:27). Within the being of every Christian there is an inner light, a voice within, which moves us toward prayer. And this inner presence is an abiding refuge in times of trial and tribulation.[2]

It was the reality of Christ in the believer that enabled the early Christians to suffer martyrdom with such joy. In A.D. 202 Septimius Severus, emperor of the Roman Empire, issued an edict outlawing the spread of Christianity. This edict was directed especially against new converts and their teachers. One new convert, Felicitas, was pregnant at the time of her arrest. She was imprisoned for many months and during that time she gave birth to a baby girl. Seeing her moan in childbirth, her jailers asked how she expected to be able to face the beasts in the arena. She answered, "Now my sufferings are only mine. But when I face the beasts, there will be *another who will live in me* and will suffer for me since I shall be suffering for Him" (italics mine).[3]

This reality of "Another living within me" was key to my healing from homosexuality, and it is key to the healing of all persons. For no matter what horrible memory came up, no matter what vile sin was revealed from within my heart, no matter what petty or ludicrous thought raced through my mind, no matter what soul-shaking pain overcame me, I now knew that Jesus was living in me. Because there was "Another living in me," I had the courage to face the beasts within the arena of my heart. That healthy place where Jesus indwelt me was my *true* center.

Becoming Mature

The Scriptures call us to embrace the lifelong process of becoming mature in Christ. In Ephesians 4:13, "until we all reach unity in the faith and in the knowledge of the Son of God and become mature, attaining to the whole measure of the fullness of Christ," the Greek word meaning "mature," teleios, is also translated as "full-grown" or "adult."[4] We do not attain full maturity at conversion nor while on this side of heaven. Rather on our journey here we keep growing up into the fullness of Christ. This growing up could also be called identification with Christ or sanctification.

Sanctification is the process of becoming holy with the ultimate goal of being like Jesus. To the Christian, all becoming is *incarnational*—it is a Life that is poured into us from on high. That Life is Jesus. For this reason all Christians, not only St. Paul, can joyfully proclaim, "It is no longer I who live, but it is Christ who lives in me" (Galatians 2:20 RSV).

The process of identification with Christ enables the believer to discover his true identity. The end product of identification is an identity—what the New English Bible calls the true self. Jesus said, "If anyone wishes to be a follower of mine, he must leave self behind; he must take up his cross and come with me. Whoever cares for his own safety is lost; but if a man will let himself be lost for my sake, he will find his true self" (Matthew 16:24, 25). While seeming to have lost himself by the world's standard, the Christian paradoxically finds his true self by following Jesus.

The true self is the result of a new created order in which human beings become children of God in the likeness of the Son of God, "the firstborn among many brothers" (Romans 8:29). The journey of life is for identification with Christ. Ultimately in glory, we shall be like him, free from sin and thoroughly pure.

> Dear friends, now we are children of God, and what we will be has not yet been made known. But we know that when he appears, we shall be like him, for we shall see him as he is. Everyone who has this hope in him purifies himself, just as he [Jesus] is pure. (1 John 3:2, 3)

Just as the true self (or the new creation) is that which is in union with Christ, the false self (or the old man) is that which is in union with Adam. However, our union with Adam is mentioned only once in the New Testament (1 Corinthians 15:22). For that reason, the Christian emphasizes the existence of the true self in union with Christ while daily dying to the false self in union with Adam. Our primary identity is that of saint, not sinner.

Empowered Obedience

As Emmanuel, Christ is God with us. As an indwelling presence, the Holy Spirit is God within us. Because God is present both with and in us, we say He is immanent, a central aspect of what it means to be a personal God. However, God can be immanent only because He is also transcendent. He is always present because He is "totally other"—unlike any created thing. Likewise, He is Lord of both Heaven and earth. As Lord over all, the Heavenly Father is that objective source Who tells us who we really are. As the Holy Spirit indwells us, God's Word has a place within our soul from which to bear fruit.

We become mature as we obey God. With our eyes off of self and directed outward toward Heaven, we receive from God that objective word we must obey if we are to mature. The true self could also be called the true "I" in every Christian. The true "I" emerges as we set our gaze on God, the true "Thou." With our eyes firmly on God (Thou), our true self (I) is reflected back to us.

Martin Buber, a Jewish scholar born in Vienna in 1878, originally articulated the theory of the "I-Thou" relationship as central to human growth. He differentiates the "I-Thou" relationship of person to person from the "I-It" relationship of person to object. According to Buber, there can only be an "I" if there is a "Thou" telling me there is an "I." "I become through my relation to the *Thou*; as I become *I*, I say *Thou*. All real living is meeting."[5]

Jesus, the one who leads us to the Father, is the one through whom the "I-Thou" relationship between humanity and God is restored. Through Christ we "become children of God—children not born of natural descent, nor of human decision or a husband's will, but born of God" (John 1:12b,13).

We cannot discover the true self by looking inward. Rather, the true self is born out of relationship to God and others. By definition, the true self is outwardly directed, as opposed to being preoccupied with the self. Looking away from the self, we are able to partake of the beautiful realities that exist outside ourselves. Those beautiful realities—such as the simplicity of a flower, the innocence of a child, or as Mother Teresa has found, the inherent dignity of every human being—begin to shape us into the people God created us to be.

The Scripture teaches that by believing in God's promises, every Christian partakes of the divine nature.

> His divine power has given to us all things that pertain to life and godliness, through the knowledge of Him who called us by glory and virtue, by which have been given to us exceedingly great and precious promises, that through these you may be partakers of the divine nature, having escaped the corruption that is in the world through lust. (2 Peter 1:3, 4 NKJV)

The Greek Orthodox Church has a well-thought-out theology of what it means to "become partakers of the divine nature." This privilege depends on redemption and issues forth from the believer's union with Christ. The Orthodox emphasize the incarnation of Christ as the powerful reality that allows the Christian believer to partake of the nature of God. Irenaeus, an early church father, viewed the incarnation not only as God coming down to man, but also as "raising man to God."[6] In Christ Jesus, God became man and partook of our nature; by believing in Him, we are given the grace to partake of His nature.

This implies that through our union with Christ we become as He was—that is, a holy, mature people—not that we become God. As Irenaeus wrote in *Against Heresies*, "[Jesus] redeemed us from the apostasy by his blood that we also might be made a holy people."[7] Athanasius put it this way, "He sanctified the body by being in it."[8] Partaking of the divine nature does not imply that we are without sin. The same Christian tradition that has given us this theology has given us the Jesus Prayer: "Lord Jesus, Son of the living God, have mercy on me, a sinner."

Partaking of the divine nature is the integral aspect of sanctification that empowers the Christian to obey God. "If anyone loves me, he will obey my teaching. My Father will love him, and we will come to him and make our home with him" (John 14:23). To abide in Christ and to partake of His nature is to have the divine power to obey. Anything less is mere human effort. Obedience is at the heart of becoming mature in Christ. We obey because His nature is within us. About this, Oswald Chambers writes:

> There is no possibility of questioning when God speaks *if He speaks to His own nature in me;* prompt obedience is the only result. When Jesus says, "Come," I simply come; when He says, "Let go," I let go; when He says, "Trust God in this matter," I do trust. The whole working out is the evidence that the nature of God is in me. (italics mine)[9]

God's nature in me redeems my nature in me. I am righteous because His righteous nature indwells me through the Holy Spirit, not simply because I know a theological truth about His righteousness in me.

From the standpoint of His nature in me, I am empowered from within to choose and to desire good. Because of Jesus' work of redemption, my desire for evil can be changed into zeal for good. "[Jesus] gave himself for us to redeem us from all wickedness and to purify for himself a people that are his very own, eager to do what is good" (Titus 2:14). Temptation for the Christian should not merely remind us that the "false self" still exists within us. Rather temptation can be an opportunity to practice the truth of Another living within us, empowering us to choose good and to fight against the evil in the world, the flesh, and the devil.

> Therefore, my dear friends, as you have always obeyed—not only in my presence, but now much more in my absence—continue to work out your salvation with fear and trembling, for *it is God who works in you to will and to act according to his good purpose.* (Philippians 2:12, 13, italics mine)

God's working in me gave me the courage to endure those first few months while I was being healed of the homosexual neurosis. Christ's presence in me is not a feeling I must conjure up; instead it is a reality that transcends my feeling being. For that reason, while my body was being ravaged with homosexual desires, I could call on Jesus in those moments when I did not feel Him near me. Without shame or guilt I waited in His presence until the ravaging desires passed. Eventually, the homosexual desires I had once eagerly sought to fulfill were transformed into temptations to do something I no longer wanted to do. Another lived in me. His righteousness in me, Christ in me, was transforming me from the inside out.

Now when I am tempted to sin, I immediately look up and out of myself and call on Jesus' name. Then I acknowledge that though I am still a sinner, my primary identity is my true self in union with Christ. From the center of that self, where I partake of God's nature, I exercise the power available to me to obey Him. I continue practicing the presence of God with me and within me until the temptation is over. In doing this, I've come to see that the duration of a temptation is limited. The more we persevere in His presence, the shorter temptations last. Never have I denied the temptations present in my body. I've merely come to acknowledge the greater reality: There is Another who lives within me and He will see me through this.

We all need to exercise moral effort in order to obey God. However, our human efforts are enhanced by God's power as we partake of His nature and daily pick up our cross and follow Jesus.

My Prayer Life

When I attended Leanne Payne's adult Christian education class, she suggested that her students begin keeping "listening-prayer" journals. Following Leanne's advice, I noted in my journal the Scriptures that I read every morning and wrote out any verses that particularly spoke to me. Often I would pray those verses to the Lord. Then I actively waited in His presence for the word He was sending back. As I waited, I frequently had a mental image of my heart leaning into the heart of Christ. For over a month I heard Him speak to me the same thing, "I love you, Mario." And for a month I faithfully wrote down in my journal these four words God spoke to me every day.

At the end of the month, I became tired of hearing the same four words, "I love you, Mario, I love you, Mario, I love you, Mario . . ." Finally I asked the Lord, "I've been hearing the same four words for over a month. Couldn't You please send me something else?"

Then I heard His reply, "You don't believe Me."

So I took those four words and quietly held them in my heart before the Lord until they sank deeply into me.

Henri Nouwen writes:

> Prayer takes place where heart speaks to heart; that is where the heart of God is united with the heart that prays. Thus knowing God becomes loving God, just as being known by God is being loved by God.[10]

It is by knowing God and *being known* by God that we encounter our heart and are freed to further identify with Christ. Because the unhealed heart can be our own worst enemy, God gradually reveals its contents to us so that we might continue to mature in Him.

> This then is how we know that we belong to the truth, and how we *set our hearts at rest in his presence*, whenever our hearts condemn us. For God is greater than our hearts, and he knows everything. (1 John 3:19, 20, italics mine)

Because God assured me early in my prayer life of His love for me, I began to trust Him to show me all that my heart really contained. It was safe for me to be known by God because I was certain of His love. This freed me to be painfully honest, vulnerable, and humble before Him.

If we sit vulnerably before God in prayer, we will encounter all the confusion and sin that has followed us into our Christian lives. There, in the presence of God, we can fearlessly let Him see those things which before our conversion we did not dare reveal. After offering these parts of our old self for God to view, we wait before Him while He transforms, heals, or equips us to destroy those parts of the old carnal self.

Cognitive psychologists are quick to point out that faulty thought patterns dictate many of the behaviors and feelings that rule our lives. These psychologists know that the introduction of new positive thoughts into a mind cluttered with diseased attitudes is key to healing. Biblical prophetic prayer or listening prayer, going, as it does, beyond positive thoughts, is key to renewing the mind:

> Do not conform any longer to the pattern of this world, but be transformed by the renewing of your mind. Then you will be able to test and approve what God's will is—his good, pleasing and perfect will. (Romans 12:2)

By waiting before God in listening prayer, we become aware of all the irrational, petty, and sinful thoughts that negatively shape us. We can objectify these negative thoughts by writing them out in our journal and then asking God to replace them with the positive recreating word of truth from the Holy Scripture or a prophetic word from God.

It was in prayer that I faced the negative attitudes, criticisms, and judgments I held against others. These thoughts prevented me from entering into close relationships with those toward whom I was most critical—particularly my fellow Christians. Finally, I wrote out these judgments of others in my prayer journal and asked God's forgiveness for them. Then I asked Him to open my eyes to see all the good qualities in these people. With God's help, I replaced my old judgmental thoughts about others with truthful positive statements about them. I wrote out these new truthful statements in my journal next to the old judgmental thoughts I had once held. This freed me to love people more fully.

Responsibility and the Will

We are dialogical creatures; we become mature as we are spoken to and respond. We who desire healing must daily put ourselves in the responsive position, expectantly waiting before God for that word that will heal us. Once we receive it, whether it is from the Scriptures, another Christian believer, worship, a good sermon, or a prophetic word we hear from God in prayer, we then have the responsibility to act on that word. Responsibility is at the heart of becoming mature in Christ Jesus.

> The Christian . . . holds that man has his essence and freedom in God's Word of creation and grace. In this act of God which is unthinkable without a responsive act of man, that is, in responsibility, man has his being. He is man through his relation to God. Outside of that relation man is a caricature of man; he is, as we can say in German, an "un-man." . . . Man is human because and in so far as he lives in the love of God and therefore in love towards his brother man.[11]

Prior to redemption, we live in a monologue. Alienated from God, we are fallen from the divine splendor and caught in a downward spiral of becoming the "un-man." It is in dialogue with our Creator that we respond to God's great initiative act of redemption through the cross of Christ. By daily making responsible choices before God, we become the best facilitators of our own healing. But our response to the cross also decides our destiny—either heaven or hell.

In order for us to make responsible choices before God, our will to choose must be intact. Exercising the will, when it is wounded, is like trying to pull our feet out of a tar pit. All strength and energy are used up in futile attempts to get free from the pit. When the will is wounded and the soul is exhausted from fighting the miry pit, a person becomes passive.

After a particularly long period of passivity, I cried out to God asking why exercising my will took such mammoth effort. I then remembered, as I related earlier, something one of my father's former employees had said to me, "Mario, your father is the only man I know who can castrate another man with a dirty look." Indeed, my father's eyes were often filled with anger, mockery, and disgust when he looked at me. I too felt castrated by his looks.

Along with my masculinity, my will was seriously wounded by him.

After realizing this, I asked Ted and Lucy Smith, fellow team members at Pastoral Care Ministries, for prayer. Ted asked God to heal all areas of my masculinity where I felt castrated by my father. Then Lucy, seeing in the Spirit, had an image of my will. "I see your will as a very thin thread that is about to snap. Let's ask Jesus to heal your will, Mario." As we prayed, Lucy saw another picture. "I see the Lord wrapping His will around your thin thread like will. His will looks like a thick golden rope being coiled around yours."

A few weeks after that prayer, I came into a new sense of responsibility for my healing, which changed my life. I still needed a lot more healing for past wounds. I had enough hurts to whine and moan about for the next twenty years. But a new dimension to life opened up—the future unencumbered by the past. Now I looked forward to a normal life free from daily references to the painful past. Because of this, I decided not to mention my past unless in the context of prayer, teaching, or ministering to others.

Some might say I went from being a victim to being a survivor. But even the word survivor held a negative connotation for me, as it was a term born out of the past. Instead, I saw myself as the new creature in Christ the Scripture said I was (2 Corinthians 5:17). More than anything, I wanted to be a worker in God's Kingdom, free from the past. For the first time, Luke 9:62 made sense to me: "No one who puts his hand to the plow and looks back is fit for service in the kingdom of God."

After the Smiths prayed with me, the debilitating passivity vanished. I have since prayed many "healing-of-the-will" prayers for persons in need of release from passivity and also in need of taking responsibility for their lives before God. The following is an example of this type of prayer:

Come, Holy Spirit. Even now, Lord Jesus, enable me to grab hold of Your outstretched hand. As I reach out my hands toward heaven and look up and out of myself, I cry out as St. Paul did, "In my weakness, O Lord, You are strong." Now, Lord, enter into my will and heal it where it has been wounded. Reveal to me any person from the past who has exhausted my will, wounded my will, or even broken my will. *(Let the Holy Spirit speak to your heart about any person who so wounded you.)* Now, Lord, give me the grace to choose to forgive that person for sinning against me. *(Name of person)*, I forgive you in Jesus' name for your sin against me. I forgive you for wounding me in my will. I will no longer be shaped by your sin against me. I look now to God to restore my will. Let Your divine power, O Lord, wrap itself around my weak, tired will; cause it to grow and to strengthen. Let my will be one with Your will, dear Heavenly Father. I thank You for doing that just now. I thank You for empowering me to obey You. I thank You, Lord, that from this day forward I will take responsibility for my life before You. Amen.

Biblical Prophetic Prayer

While the Bible is God's Word for all people and is applicable to every human heart, God, through the Holy Spirit, speaks prophetic words to the individual believer in prayer—words applicable only to that individual. The New Testament believer is in a far better place to receive a prophetic word from God than the Old Testament believer was. In the Old Testament only prophets and Israel's national leaders were given the Holy Spirit. In the New Testament, all believers may receive Him.

The great prophecy in the Book of Joel is that in the Day of the Lord:

> I will pour out my Spirit on all people. Your sons and daughters will prophesy, your old men will dream dreams, your young men will see visions. Even on my servants, both men and women, I will pour out my Spirit in those days. (Joel 2:28, 29)

In Acts chapter two, Peter announces that Joel 2:28, 29 was fulfilled in the giving of the Holy Spirit at Pentecost. At that time, the Holy Spirit came to dwell in all of God's people. Prior to Pentecost, the Holy Spirit only rested on a few of God's people. This is the essential change in the role of the Holy Spirit between the Old and New Testaments.

In the Old Testament, the prophet was one who heard from the Lord as a result of the Spirit of God resting upon him. The Spirit of God and the prophetic utterance were inextricably linked. In both the Old Testament and New Testament prophecy is nothing more than rightly hearing the voice of God in the presence of His Spirit.

Therefore, when Paul in 1 Corinthians 14:1 and 14:39 encourages all believers in Corinth to be eager to prophesy, he is exhorting them to move in the gift of rightly hearing God's voice. The New Testament gift of prophecy is for all believers because all believers partake of God's Spirit. Prophetic prayer is nothing more than taking hold of God's outstretched hand. Donald Bloesch writes:

> I agree with the prophets and the Reformers that the essence of prayer is not a mystical lifting up of the mind to God but the descent of the Spirit into our hearts (cf. Isa. 45:8; 64:1; Ps. 42:8; 144:5–7; Ezek. 2:1, 2; Zech. 12:10). It is not climbing the mystical ladder to heaven but taking hold of the outstretched hand of God (cf. Isa. 64:7).[12]

Through His covenants with His people, the Bible, and the Holy Spirit, God stretches out His hand and initiates conversation with us. Our job is to grab hold of His outstretched hand, speak back to Him, and then expectantly wait for His reply. We can wait expectantly because we believe that our God is a listening Father. The Psalmist puts it this way, "In the morning, O LORD, you hear my voice; in the morning I lay my requests before you and wait in expectation" (Psalm 5:3). Bernhard W. Anderson, writing about active waiting before God, says:

> In these contexts, the verb wait expresses a straining toward the future, a keen anticipation of what is to come. Hope is waiting with one's whole being for the dawn when the re-creating word of forgiveness will be spoken (Ps. 130:5–6); it is waiting eagerly for Yahweh the King to come in saving power.[13]

Prayer is the way in which we have our daily meeting with God. As Martin Buber has said, "All real living is meeting." We become mature by actively waiting for that "re-creating word" from God that affirms us as new creatures in Christ. About receiving that word from God, Emil Brunner says:

> If it be true that man has his essence in responsibility, that is, in being addressed by God, or if, as they used to say formerly, man is created after the image of God, it is evident that man can be *himself* only in receiving the divine Word.[14]

Through our conversations with Him, God will speak to us about the sins, both our own or those of others, which bind us and prevent us from further identification with Christ. Once these sins are revealed, we are free to receive God's remedy for release from them. We choose to repent and ask forgiveness for ourselves, or we acknowledge the sins of others against us and choose to forgive them before God. The more we are released from our own sins and those of others, the more our true self comes forth.

God's word always asks for a response from us. Have you ever noticed how many "if" statements Jesus makes in the Gospels? These statements are conditional. In Matthew 19:17 Jesus says, "If you want to enter life, obey the commandments." In Mark 9:35 Jesus says, "If anyone wants to be first, he must be the very last, and the servant of all." In John 13:17 Jesus, talking about acts of servanthood, tells His disciples, "You will be blessed, if you do them." These promises call us into dialogue with God. Their fulfillment depends on whether we choose to meet the conditions. Oswald Chambers relates this principle to discipleship:

> God brings us to a standard of life by His grace, and we are responsible for reproducing that standard in others. . . . Whenever our Lord talked about discipleship, He always prefaced it with an "IF," never with an emphatic assertion—"You must." Discipleship carries an option with it.[15]

Not only is prayer our daily meeting with God, it is also our daily meeting with ourselves. There in His presence, we can objectively see with His eyes all that is within our hearts. We must be willing to die to all the foolishness and sin that resides within us if we are to become all that God created us to be. Finally, it is in prayer that we receive from God those affirming words that edify us and encourage us to grow more into the image of Christ.

6

Loving the Same Sex

And Jonathan made a covenant with David
because he loved him as himself. Jonathan took
off the robe he was wearing and gave it to
David, along with his tunic, and even his sword,
his bow and his belt.

1 Samuel 18:3, 4

Rightly Loving versus Wrongly Loving

Shortly after coming out of the closet, I moved to New York City to attend acting school. I lived in a neighborhood known as the East Village. Stenciled in shocking pink, graffiti on the sidewalks warned, "CLONES, GO HOME." While walking down the street with a gay friend, I asked him, "Who are the Clones?"

"They're West Village gays. You know who they are; they're the gays who all dress and look alike."

Clones really did all look alike. A typical Clone had very short hair, a moustache, and a pumped-up body. They wore mirrored sunglasses, a white T-shirt or tank top, a tight pair of Levi button fly jeans, and clunky shoes. In the winter, most Clones wore leather bomber jackets.

Clones tended to date one another. A boisterous lesbian friend of mine, while walking through the West Village, sarcastically asked a Clone couple in Sheridan Square, "What's it like, having sex with yourself?" Her question stayed with me for years. Clones' dress and body type were exaggerated symbols of maleness. The hyper masculine image they projected was their idealized and eroticized view of the same sex. Their external image of maleness served as a psychological defense against the internal deficit of masculinity. In lieu of real masculine love, attainable only through nonerotic means, they tried to encounter the masculine through an external image of masculinity in themselves and their same-sex partners.

The love expressed between homosexuals is in stark contrast to the love between healthy heterosexual men. In the Bible Jonathan and David are a prime example of the giving love that marks healthy relating between heterosexual men. Jonathan's love for David was predicated on Jonathan's love for himself. This Biblical self-love is not to be confused with narcissistic self-centered love. Rather Biblical self-love could be equated with self-acceptance. Because Jonathan rightly loved and accepted himself, he could rightly love and accept another like himself.

The love between Jonathan and David was characterized by giving. Under the leading of the Lord, Jonathan freely relinquished his right to succeed his father as king of Israel. Out of love, Jonathan gave his right to the throne to David. Some scholars believe that in giving David his robe, Jonathan recognized "that David was to assume his place as successor to Saul."[1]

The love between homosexuals is often characterized by taking. The homosexual does not love another of the same sex to give of himself. Rather the homosexual loves another to take for himself. The homosexual does not love the same-sex partner as himself. He loves the partner instead of himself.

Same-Sex Ambivalence

The ambivalent coexistence of both love and hate is a central element of homosexual neurosis. In psychology the word ambivalence refers to the existence of contradictory attitudes or emotions, such as love and hate, in the same individual or to rapidly shifting or alternating emotional attitudes toward another.[2]

In homosexuality, both men and women may be the objects of this love-hate ambivalence. Throughout childhood development we view the sexes as they relate to each other. We experience maleness and femaleness as two sides of the same coin, that coin being humanity. Therefore, if because of inadequate models we have difficulty relating to persons of the same sex, we also have difficulty relating to persons of the other sex. In this chapter we deal with same-sex ambivalence. The next two chapters will address other-sex ambivalence.

The homosexual condition results in part from not receiving needed love from our own gender, usually the same-sex parent. To defend ourselves from the loss of this same-sex love, we detach in an unhealthy way from that parent. In the child's mind this detachment might take the form of a vow, "You don't love me; I am not going to love you either."

Broken relationships with the same sex imprint on the deep heart confused images of that sex. Additionally, our hearts' images of those who hurt or rejected us as children are further darkened by our sinful responses to their offenses against us. These heart images contain all the negative feelings and attitudes linked to our broken same-sex relationships.

Our hearts' images of significant same-sex others dictate how we relate to the same sex. Present-day difficulties in relating to the same sex often arise from broken same-sex relationships from the past. Defensive detachment from the same-sex parent may become a generalized detachment from all that parent symbolized to us. In our pain, we unconsciously project onto all members of the same sex our diseased feelings and attitudes. While erotically charged love may flow out of us toward someone of our own sex, so may repressed hatred, anger, or rejection. The unconscious projections of same-sex ambivalence are unpredictable. For the homosexual (or lesbian), certain people may elicit more ambivalence than others, simply because these people symbolize some aspect of his (or her) own sex which he (or she) is alienated from or confused about.

Deep inside the heart of the homosexual (or lesbian) may be two polarized images of the same sex. In one corner of the heart reigns the idealized romantic image of the same sex—how the heart symbolizes the neurotic love he (or she) feels for the same sex. This image may be of the perfect same-sex parent or the perfect homosexual (or lesbian) lover. In the other corner of the homosexual's (lesbian's) heart reigns the feared, despised image of the same sex—how the heart symbolizes the neurotic hatred he (or she) feels for the same sex. For the homosexual, perhaps this is an image of a cruel authoritarian or passive absent father. For the lesbian, this may be an image of the distant unloving or abused passive mother. Between these two extremes of the idealized image and the despised image may be a variety of distorted images of the same sex.

The Perfect Lover

An idealized and eroticized image of the same sex plays a large part in homosexual relationships. When in love, the homosexual is really enamored with his heart's idealized image of his own sex. The same-sex partner merely matches this idealized image, as exemplified in the story of the Clones. The homosexual's relationship with his same-sex partner is based more on a projection of an illusory image from his heart than on real love for another person.

Part of my healing from homosexuality came only when I renounced the idolatrous *hope* of someday finding that perfect homosexual lover who matched my heart's idealized and eroticized image of the same sex. After receiving deep healing from the Lord, I still had this idolatrous hope in my heart. I knew this was an ungodly hope and that I needed to die to it. But I still wanted some control of my life. In my mind I still believed there might be a man in this world who could fulfill my needs. At this point, the homosexual neurosis was no longer anxiously clamoring within me. It was now more a quiet neurotic hum. Now Satan's temptation to me was to take the healing Jesus had given me thus far and to seek out that perfect homosexual lover with whom to quietly spend the rest of my life.

That sinful hope was a major block to my receiving further healing from God. After I repented, I faced the reality that in my initial turning from homosexuality I had left something I found great pleasure in. The Bible speaks of the "pleasures of sin" (Hebrews 11:25). Part of the reason why we fail to remain free from certain sins is our denial that these sins contain an element of pleasure. During this period as I struggled to remain free from homosexual activity, I daily reminded myself that I had given to God something I liked. I also asked God to replace my yearnings for these carnal pleasures with a sincere longing for good and holy pleasures. For quite a while, my prayer to God was, "Open my eyes to see the good and holy things You've placed in this world. Open my heart to respond with love, joy, and wonderment at these things."

Another factor in homosexual relationships is the search for gender identity through the same-sex partner. Men who failed to complete their gender identification in childhood seek to establish it in another. The overwhelming feeling of being "in love" with someone of the same sex is actually a quest for gender identification that has become eroticized.

When a person with a homosexual neurosis seeks healing, the caregiver must find out if he is involved in an ongoing homosexual relationship. Separation from the same-sex partner may unearth the pain of incomplete gender identification. In a homosexual relationship such pain may be temporarily repressed.

In order to be healed, the homosexual must face this inner void and acknowledge that he tried to fill it with an idealized and eroticized image of the same sex—that this void caused him to posit his identity in another of the same sex. This amounts to having set up the same sex as an idol in his heart.

The prophet Ezekiel tells us that in our separation from God we have set up idols (Ezekiel 14:7). Romans 1:18–23 tells us that the wrath of God has come against all humanity, not just the homosexual, because of idolatry. We "exchanged the glory of the immortal God for images made to look like mortal man." Within the context of Romans 1, homosexuality is mentioned as one of the results of mankind's idolatry (Romans 1:26, 27). In order to be healed, the homosexual must repent of his idolatry. But the church must also understand how this sin relates to the homo-sexual's need for deep healing in his gender identity. In the church we need an environment of grace where a void created by incom-plete gender identification may be ministered to with great patience and genuine love.

The Despised Image

While active in the gay lifestyle, I worked as a waiter in many restaurants. One restaurant was not doing well when I first started there. The owner, in an attempt to save his failing busi-ness, hired an experienced restaurateur to manage the dining room. When I first met Mr. Winston, I liked him. He was a stately man with graying hair and a charming smile. He had a certain elegance about him, and I was even slightly sexually attracted to him.

Under Mr. Winston's management, the dining room of the restaurant was restructured so that each waiter had one fewer table to serve. From a management perspective, Mr. Winston rea-soned that with fewer tables to serve the waiters would have more time for each customer. As service improved, so would business. From my perspective as a waiter, this meant making less money. Immediately, my feelings for Mr. Winston made a one-hundred-eighty-degree turn. My liking for him turned into intense dislike. From that point on, I perceived him to be a controlling older man and a threat to my livelihood.

The other extreme view the heart may hold of the same sex is the despised image. This image may be a composite of same-sex persons who have wounded us in the past. When someone suf-fering with homosexuality seeks healing, he may for the first time become aware that he has problems relating to authority figures. This is easily understood as parents provide our first encounters with authority figures. If we fail to see these authority figures as benevolent, we may see all authority figures as malevolent.

With hindsight I can see I projected onto Mr. Winston my mis-trust and dislike for male authority figures. This projection was rooted in my broken relationship with my father. Mr. Winston and my father were alike in two basic ways. First, they were both older. Second, they both exercised authority over me. I had no objectivity toward authority figures and could not see Mr. Winston's reasoning behind his decision.

Subjective feeling reactions are a hallmark of same-sex ambivalence. Rather than objectively seeing Mr. Winston's action from his managerial perspective, I subjectively reacted from my pool of ambivalent feelings toward older men. I attributed almost diabolical motives to him and reacted very defensively. One moment he was an attractive, stately gentleman to me; the next moment he just was another threatening authority figure trying to control and destroy me. However, in the end the restructuring improved our business, and as a result my income increased. But that did not matter to me. Although I came to see some good in his accomplishment, I continued to react to him subjectively until the day I left that restaurant.

We may despise entire categories of people simply because some person from that category rejected us in childhood. As a child my giftedness in the arts drew me to this area. Some of my male classmates viewed my interests as girlish, and they ridiculed me. These boys were the "jocks," the athletes. In adulthood, long after my healing was well underway, the Lord led me to forgive one particularly cruel classmate and then to repent of my negative attitudes toward all men who loved sports.

Paranoia and Same-Sex Ambivalence

Freud is credited for first connecting paranoia to male homosexuality. Commenting on Freud's analysis of paranoia and male homosexuality, Dr. William Niederland writes:

> The familiar principal forms of paranoia can all be represented as contradictions of the single proposition: "I (a man) *love* him (a man)." This is changed to "I do not love him—I *hate* him." Still unacceptable in this form, the feeling expressed in the second statement is projected onto the one originally loved. Consequently the proposition "I hate *him*" is transformed via projection into the idea "he hates *me* and is persecuting *me*," such change providing the inner justification for "*hating him*."[3]

The change from "I love him" to "I hate him" constitutes the same love-hate dynamic found in same-sex ambivalence in homosexuality. Dr. Frank Lake in his book *Clinical Theology* lists several adjectives that characterize paranoia. These are especially applicable to the homosexual condition—"defensive, opinionated, suspicious of detractors, wary of critics; always 'establishing' his position against those who seem to be encroaching on his rights, litigious, argumentative."[4]

While living in New York City, I was briefly involved in a gay political theater group. We produced plays for gays, by gays, about gays. A strong "them and us" mentality pervaded this group. "Them" referred to the oppressive homophobic heterosexuals who ran the world. We poor, persecuted gays were trapped in a straight world. Historically, society and the church have treated homosexual people as less than persons and as objects of hatred. In today's homosexual community this persecution has wrought a generalized paranoia, which is manifested by militant gays and lesbians crying loudly for their rights. Militant gay groups lobby government officials with a litigious and argumentative expertise unmatched by any other special interest group.

Both a sense of being persecuted and a fighting posture are hallmarks of homosexual paranoia. When I attributed diabolical motives to Mr. Winston, I expressed a paranoid reaction. I fought his decision to restructure the dining room by going to upper management and litigating against him. Posturing like a lawyer in a courtroom, I believed I had a case, and I was prepared to fight for my rights.

Mistrust and suspicion are two other major elements in homosexual paranoia. Many years after overt homosexual attraction ceased to be an issue with me, I found myself continuing to mistrust men. This mistrust formed a major barrier to my establishing healthy same-sex friendships. When I encountered men with issues of control, I often reacted with an anger that wounded them, rather than objectively dealing with their controlling behavior. My anger was an immature way of establishing my boundaries and coming free from their control. These angry reactions were psychological transferences rooted in my father's crushing control over me.

Finally, the voice of the "self-pitying child" at the center of the homosexual neurosis is akin to the litigating voice in homosexual paranoia. This voice fights and defends the inner child's right to complain. Dr. Gerard van den Aardweg writes:

> It looks as if the "inner child" fights for his position of being *important-tragic* and fears that he may lose this addictive form of self-love. We can understand what Freud meant when he discussed the phenomenon of resistance he observed in the treatment of many neurotics and which made on him "the deepest impression of all," giving him "the feeling that there is a force at work that defends itself with all possible means against cure and that obstinately clings to illness and sufferings."[5]

Healing from homosexual paranoia came to me as, first, I learned to test all my negative thinking about the same sex. Instead of accepting every negative thought, I held it in my heart before God. In my prayer journal, I wrote out all the things I held against the men I knew. Then I asked God to show me whether these negative thoughts were true or false.

Second, I learned not to live from my center of negative thoughts and feelings. Initially, this meant learning to live in the tension of two opposing centers—the old center of the neurotic self which I was dying to daily and the new center of my true redeemed self in Christ which I was coming more alive to every day. I did not allow the voice of the paranoid self-pitying inner child to dominate me. Rather, I starved his complaining, critical voice by practicing the presence of Christ in me. The indwelling presence of the Holy Spirit and God's living Word, the Scriptures, constituted my true center. Dr. Lake in his book *Clinical Theology* tells how he helped his paranoid patients to develop a "double orientation." He taught them to live in the tension of two opposing centers, but to let the truthful nonparanoid center dominate. Dr. Lake found this to be central to healing these persons.

Third, on those occasions when a negative thought about someone of the same sex proved to be accurate, I learned not to speak it out. Of course, I often failed, but over a period of time, I became successful at keeping these criticisms to myself. Eventually, I learned to give any accurate criticisms about others to the Lord in prayer. This is not to say that I denied these character flaws in others existed. I simply decided not to let them become my definitive view of others.

Fourth, and perhaps most important, I looked for the good in another person and verbally commended it whenever possible. In a fallen world it is easy to see what's wrong with others, as the Biblical parable of the man with the log in his eye so beautifully tells us. But it is truly virtuous to look for the good in others and accentuate that good.

Same-Sex Ambivalence and Anger

When twenty-five years of repressed anger toward my own sex came up from within me, it was downright scary. Over a period of several months, attacks of anger lasting for several hours at a time would overtake me. These attacks occurred as I came out of denial about the dysfunction in my family. Awakening in the middle of the night, I would find my teeth grinding in fury while a knot of anger and anxiety churned away in my gut. Knowing better than to deny the emotion, I just let it be. This was the anger I had previously internalized and that had been the root of much of my black depression, self-hatred, and suicidal thoughts.

Often my anger was directed toward a man who was also the recipient of my same-sex ambivalence. In some instances, fury and sensuality intermingled within me (remember, ambivalence means the presence of *both* distorted love and hatred). Though I may have had minor reason to be annoyed with the man, the amount of anger was all out of proportion to the situation.

Dr. John Bancroft in *Human Sexuality and Its Problems* has written, "Anger may facilitate sexual response." He tells of two psychological studies showing that "inducing anger leads to greater sexual imagery."[6] Just as anxiety and lust are related, so too anger and lust are related. To responsibly deal with anger is to find relief from lust and related sexual imagery (such as a diseased sexual fantasy life). Pulling out the underlying root of anger toward the same sex from the deep heart helps to disengage homo-erotic imagery and homosexual responses lodged there.

While I didn't deny my angry feelings, I did have to deal with them. The first principle in overcoming anger is to stop projecting it onto others. I had to own my anger.

Then I prayed. The best place to be angry is in God's presence. With my arms lifted up to Jesus, I could see Him on the cross dying to take all my sins into His body. My anger seemed like a black current of thick smoke flowing up through my body and escaping through my hands as if it were being drawn out of me and into the wounds of Jesus.

Certain other actions also helped. I went for long bicycle rides along secluded paths, screaming at the top of my lungs. I wrote in my prayer journal all the negative, petty, ludicrous thoughts I had toward the objects of my anger and same-sex ambivalence. I wrote letters that I never intended to send to the objects of my anger.

I laughed at myself, especially when the voice of the whiny, self-pitying inner child emerged along with the anger. Dramatizing his plight helped to silence him: "Oh, you poor hurting child, never before in the history of the world has there been anyone who deserved to be more angry than you are."

I removed from my vocabulary phrases such as, "You made me angry." The real truth is that I respond to certain situations with anger, which is sometimes appropriate. But there is no one inside me, other than myself, who is *making* me angry.

I asked for prayer with the laying on of hands from trusted Christian brothers and sisters after or even during these times of deep anger.

In my anger, God did not reject me, nor did He allow me to indulge in my anger. Most important, I knew better than to project my anger onto God or to blame Him for my present circumstance. After all, He had given me Jesus, the remedy to my pain.

When I have dealt with others with this problem, I have found that sometimes a demonic 'spirit of anger' uses the pain of legitimate anger as an occasion to oppress the individual. Once discerned, that demonic presence is easily put to flight by rebuking it.

If the person has sinned against someone in anger, then he or she must go and ask their forgiveness. However, many people do not know how to deal with another person's anger. Many Christians are quick to label all anger as sin and fail to see the many times the Scripture speaks of legitimate anger.

As I dealt with my anger and stopped projecting it onto men around me, I experienced less and less homosexual temptation. As the anger diminished, so too did the related lust.

Sexualized Hatred

On many occasions, I have prayed with men whose negative side of ambivalence has become eroticized. In these cases, lust is mixed with hatred. Images of hurting or even murdering the same-sex partner(s) appear in their sexual fantasies. They always have great shame and guilt about these fantasies, and I may be the only person to whom they have ever revealed this problem. These suffering souls need to be released first from the shame and guilt. We would take care of that in a prayer session such as the following.

After invoking the name of Jesus, we then discuss the meaning these images of hurting the same sex might hold. Again, insight into symbolic confusion is the first step in disengaging the power of the neurotic imagery and its associated feelings. As we talk about the images themselves, I ask, "What do you think is the *meaning* of this imagery in your sexual fantasy?"

They often say, "A lot of lust, anger, and hatred toward that person."

"Yes, anger and hatred are most definitely affecting your inner view of the same sex. But please remember that those persons who appear in your fantasy represent masculinity to you. You must learn to take these images figuratively and not as the literal yearnings of your heart. The images of hurting and even murdering your sexual partners is how your heart symbolizes your eroticized anger and hatred toward your own sex."

Once they understand their symbolic confusion as a linking of lustful images with feelings of anger and hatred, the fear of actually living out the sexual fantasy diminishes.

I then ask if they feel they could bring this fantasy before the Lord Jesus in prayer. They almost always say yes. After invoking the name of Jesus and entering into the healing presence of God, I ask them to allow the full sexual fantasy to come to mind in His presence.

Together we then ask Jesus to enter into every perverted image in the sexual fantasy. In order to disengage these images from their deep hearts, I first ask them, "Do you repent of the lust that has become entwined with your anger and hatred?"

"Yes, I repent of that lust."

Then I ask them to pull from their minds, one by one, each diseased sexual act and symbol contained in their sexual fantasy. As they give these to Jesus in prayer, I encourage them. "Describe in detail to the Lord all the meaning this aspect of your sexual fantasy holds for you. Tell Him also all the feelings this elicits from you." We continue praying until every detail of the sexual fantasy has been given to the Lord.

Sometimes demonic spirits use this symbolic confusion to oppress or inhabit the person. It is not uncommon to have a demon manifest during the prayer time. In some cases, the demons do not manifest but simply hide. Then the gift of discerning spirits comes into play (1 Corinthians 12:10), and hiding demons can be quietly cast out. It is easy to cast out demons by asking the infested individual to renounce the demons and then by anointing the person with holy water.

Same-Sex Ambivalence and Envy

Envy, listed among the seven capital sins, is another factor in same-sex ambivalence and in homosexuality (where it is eroticized). Andrew Comiskey in *The Guidebook to Pursuing Sexual Wholeness* writes:

> We are envious of those who possess what we want but perceive we personally lack, be it on an emotional or physical level. Envy extends its impulsive, needy claws and finds a focus. This is not imitating those we admire, or developing a friendship of healthy complements; rather, envy involves an immature attempt to become mature or whole through another. This translates homosexually as one unsure of his gender and overall acceptability finds an idealized mirror in another of the same sex.[7]

Envy is related to the cannibal compulsion in homosexual neurosis. Both envy and the cannibal compulsion are directed toward those persons who symbolize to us the wholeness we are seeking in our gender identity. As quoted earlier, Dr. Ruth Tiffany Barnhouse in her book *Homosexuality: A Symbolic Confusion* remarks:

> The homosexual adaptation may be resorted to in order to identify with the "masculine" strength of the partner. As one patient of mine expressed it, "It was not so much that I wanted to love Peter; I wanted to be Peter."[8]

True to the assessment of homosexuality in the Book of Romans, both Rev. Comiskey and Dr. Barnhouse find the homosexual to be "full of envy" (Romans 1:26–29).

Many persons without homosexual neurosis are unaffirmed and insecure in their gender and sexual identity. Like the homosexual, these persons also fall into the sin of envy toward members of the same sex who symbolize wholeness in their gender. They may need to negate the good in another or to look for something negative in that person and accentuate that. When envy acknowledges the good in another, it does so only to greedily possess, control, or destroy that good. The Gospel of Matthew tells us that Jesus was handed over to Pilate because of the envy of the same crowd that later yelled, "Crucify him!" (Matthew 27:18, 22b).

We may even despise the object of our envy for having qualities we so badly want for ourselves. When envy is eroticized, either in homosexuality or in heterosexuality, it is not uncommon to simultaneously despise and be sexually attracted by the same person. When not eroticized, envy may cause a constant comparing of the self to others or an unhealthy sense of competition.

Sometimes envy has a demonic source. In one church tradition demonic envy has been called "evil eye"—defined as "jealousy and envy of some people for the things they do not have: beauty, youth, courage, or any other happiness."[9] Father Stephanou, a Greek Orthodox priest, writes that "satanic powers influence evil upon man through certain people."[10] He recounts how he was personally affected when he was the object of another person's demonic envy:

I was so oppressed and laid so low that I couldn't get up from the floor to get my Euchologian and stole from my car which was parked below in front of the building. I barely managed to struggle down the stairs to my car and up again to my room. I thought I would die. I could hardly muster the strength needed to open my mouth to utter the prayer of exorcism.[11]

At times when I have been the object of someone's envy, I have observed a kind of evil in that person's gaze at me. Sometimes I have felt extremely drained and even oppressed by such people. Demonic envy often comes against the very giftedness in a Christian that God intends to use for the advancement of His Kingdom. In some way the envy seems to prevent the Christian from using this God-given giftedness in its fullest potential. But the Christian has a weapon to use against this attack—the exorcism prayer. Here is an abridged version of one such prayer. (Take note that "manliness" is listed in this prayer as a characteristic envied by others. The man struggling with homosexuality often envies the manliness in another male.)

O Lord, our God, the King of the ages . . . He who creates and transforms all things by merely willing it . . . the physician and healer of our souls, the security of all those who hope in Thee, we beseech and we beg: banish, drive off and take away every diabolic action, every satanic attack and assault, evil curiosity and harm and the spell of the evil eye caused by malevolent and evil men from your servant *[Name of Person]*, and if this has occurred of beauty, or manliness, or prosperity or jealousy and envy, or evil eye, Thou Master . . . stretch forth Thy mighty hand . . . visit him [or her] with a peaceful angel, a mighty guardian of body and soul who will rebuke and drive off from him [or her] every evil design, every sorcery and spell of the evil eye of corrupting and envious men. . . .[12]

When we are guilty of envy, confession and repentance at the foot of the cross brings the healing. After repentance, it is good to thank God aloud for all the good qualities that we previously envied in the person. From that point, we can painfully acknowledge before the Lord, and others as need be, the deep sense of personal insecurity within ourselves that caused us to envy the good in another. At the base of our insecurity will be self-hatred. That too must be repented of as the sin that it is.

We may then ask God to give us the grace, discipline, and patience with the self to develop the qualities we heretofore envied in another. However, just as important, we may need to accept the fact that we may never possess those qualities. In either case, we must honor that person for the good qualities, and this is the opposite of envy.

Warning Signs of Same-Sex Ambivalence

Because the nature of same-sex ambivalence is unconscious, we need to learn to recognize its signals within us. We can ask ourselves these questions. Am I:

—experiencing envy toward,
—angry for no logical reason with,
—despising yet sexually attracted to,
—experiencing contradictory emotions toward, someone of the same sex?

And we can check our dreams. Objects of same-sex ambivalence may appear in our dreams as symbols of our gender. It is not unusual to dream about being sexually joined with one of these persons in an erotic attempt to take the good qualities we envy in the person.

A positive reply to any of the above questions may indicate that we are experiencing some ambivalence toward that person. Identification of this problem is half the battle.

My Healing from Same-Sex Ambivalence

Just as I projected onto older men unresolved issues about my father, so too did I project the issues onto God the Father. My heart's image of fatherhood needed to be radically resymbolized so that I might receive love from my Heavenly Father. And this did happen. In June of 1984, I attended an Exodus International

Conference in Baltimore, Maryland. Exodus is an umbrella organization for Christian ministries of sexual redemption for the homosexual.

The keynote speaker for the conference was Dr. Robert Frost, author of *Our Heavenly Father*. For an entire week, Dr. Frost taught on the fatherhood of God. At the end of the week, he asked Christian leaders and counselors to come forward to help him minister God's fatherly love. Then Dr. Frost asked all in the audience who needed to receive a healing touch from their Heavenly Father to come forward and receive prayer from one of the leaders. Nearly the entire audience came forward.

Dr. Frost directed us to lay our heads on the shoulders of the ones praying for us and to receive fatherly hugs from them. The minute I did this, I began to cry deeply. Soon the entire room was filled with the sobs of unaffirmed men and women receiving love from their Heavenly Father. The sobbing seemed to go on for a long time. Then a heavenly peace descended, and a quietness filled the room. The cries of the unaffirmed stopped.

Returning to my seat, I had an inner quietness I had never known before. I experienced Zephaniah 3:17 that day: "The LORD your God is with you, he is mighty to save. He will take great delight in you, he will quiet you with his love, he will rejoice over you with singing." For the first time in my life I believed that God is a real Father who genuinely delights in me and loves me. Through Dr. Frost's ministry, I received from my Heavenly Father some of the affirmation I had always longed for from my earthly father.

But even after receiving such a deep healing from God, I continued hoping to find within the Christian community a man through whom some of my legitimate same-sex love needs from childhood could be met. No longer was I searching for the perfect lover (the idealized and eroticized image of the same sex), nor was I looking for the perfect father (a noneroticized but still idealized image of the same sex); I simply wanted to find a spiritual father in the Lord as Paul had been to Timothy (1 Timothy 1:18). But the brokenness I saw in many men within the church quickly ended my search. Many of these men were as unaffirmed in their masculinity as I had been in mine, although they had not eroticized their same-sex relationships. In their attempts to receive unmet same-sex love needs, I saw some of these men doing the emotional equivalent of backward flips to get the love and approval of other men.

Finally, I ended my search for a spiritual father. If I were to be a healthy Christian man, then my primary need was to learn to relate to men as my friends and brothers in the Lord. One day in prayer, I gave to the Lord all the expectations I had of Christian men and determined to give more of myself.

This act freed me to honor older and wiser Christian men without expecting them to meet all my unmet needs for fatherly love. In these men I found models of benevolent authority, modern day heroes to emulate. Some of these men I knew personally, such as Ted Smith from Pastoral Care Ministries, Rev. Joseph Garlington from Covenant Church of Pittsburgh, Dr. Robert Frost, and my male professors from Trinity Episcopal School for Ministry in Ambridge, Pennsylvania. Others I never met personally, but I have either heard them speak or read their books. They include C. S. Lewis, Fr. Michael Scanlon from the Franciscan University at Steubenville, Ohio, and theologian Dr. Donald Bloesch. Men of great integrity, they have spoken the truth in love, carried themselves with humility, and boldly proclaimed the gospel of Christ. By honoring the good qualities in these men and modeling my true self after them, I took into myself the healthy masculinity I had always longed for. I consider these men to be my spiritual fathers.

Scripture teaches that we are not to call any man on earth father because we have one Father who is in heaven (Matthew 23:9). Had I kept trying to get all my same-sex love needs met via human relationships, my gaze would have forever been on the creature and not on the Creator. My hunger for a father was ravenous. Had a man offered to reparent me as a substitute father, I would have emotionally devoured him. Only my Heavenly Father could provide me with the healing and masculine affirmation I so desperately needed and wanted.

There is no healing for same-sex ambivalence apart from entering into nonerotic same-sex relationships. Within the context of these relationships the issues related to same-sex ambivalence inevitably surface. If the local church is not equipped to understand and deal with same-sex ambivalence in the person being healed of homosexuality, he might join a therapeutic group such as Andy Comiskey's Living Waters. This program is an excellent way to learn new relational skills to transfer into same-sex relationships in the church. If there is no local group, this program can be worked through on one's own using the book *Pursuing Sexual Wholeness*, along with the *Guidebook to Pursuing Sexual Wholeness*, available at Christian bookstores.

When it functions as a therapeutic community where understanding, forgiveness, and love flow, the church is the perfect environment for dealing with same-sex ambivalence. Such was the case at my church when these issues came flooding forward from deep within me.

After receiving that incredible healing from rejection (described in chapter 2), I became particularly aware of my same-sex ambivalence toward all the men in my Bible study group. On occasion I had unknowingly projected onto these Christian brothers my hatred and general contempt (anger) for all those persons in the past who had rejected me and my family.

Because these men expressed much love and concern for me, I knew I could confess my sin to them. But when I tried to do that, they had difficulty hearing it. Being loving Christians, they were too quick to offer forgiveness and failed to see that I needed the healing that comes from confessing and repenting of sin. "Confess your sins to each other and pray for each other so that you may be healed" (James 5:16). Our church did not often practice formal confessions. I had to beg them to hear mine.

When I eventually convinced them, great healing came to us all. Immediately after my confession, they began to confess their sins against me and against others struggling with homosexuality (to whom they had failed to reach out). Together in prayer, we extended to one another forgiveness. While in that prayer, something extraordinary happened. A stream of supernatural love flowed from me to them. Once again the simple gospel truth of confession and the forgiveness of sin was setting love in order.

We need to learn to remain before God in prayer and listen to His direction for all healing, as He may have a custom-made solution for each situation. It is not always appropriate for someone to confess same-sex ambivalence to the objects of it. They may not be committed to the person as brothers (or sisters) in Christ. They may not be mature enough to handle the confession, much less understand homosexuality. If immature, they may forever see the one confessing as "the person with the homosexual problem" and fail to relate to him as the redeemed Christian he really is.

Dealing with Temptation

As my healing progressed, with the Lord's help I worked through my same-sex ambivalence. Soon my homosexual desires, which I had previously enjoyed, were transformed into sinful temptations that I wanted less and less. While these desires eventually ended, I still faced temptations—both sexual and non-sexual. Now it was easy to discern if these sexual temptations came from "the world, the flesh, or the devil." Whatever the source, the practice of the presence of Christ indwelling my heart through faith was always the starting point to my defense.

If the temptation came from the world, I had to resist it or flee from it. A friend of mine visiting from another country remarked to me, "The men in the billboard advertisements in America are seductively posed the same way women in my country are seductively posed in our advertisements." His statement opened my eyes to see how bombarded we are here with seductive images of both men and women—especially in television and movies. As a result, I decided for my mental well-being, I would not watch television programs and movies with sexually explicit scenes.

If sexual temptations came from my flesh, these often appeared in the context of a same-sex relationship. In prayer I asked God certain key questions about the person. What is it in him that I want for myself? Do I envy him in any way? Do I feel inferior to him? Almost always, a need for more healing of my gender identity was the remedy. These temptations could be overcome by praying for more personal healing or receiving such prayer from trusted Christians.

Sexual temptation from the devil often came as thoughts invading my consciousness from outside myself. One night just before a large healing mission with Pastoral Care Ministries, I lay awake nearly the entire night as memories of past homosexual encounters raced through my head. Knowing that these were not the desires of my heart, I dismissed these memories just as quickly as they entered into my mind. But the flood of homo-erotic memories seemed endless. Finally, I took out my holy water, blessed my bedroom, and commanded the devil to stop pestering me. Then in my spirit I heard him accusingly say, "You enjoyed every one of these encounters."

Remembering only the first part of Matthew 5:25 (KJV), "Agree with thine adversary quickly," I replied, "You bet I did. But I was an unholy, neurotic man back then. Now I am becoming a healthy, holy man. Now I've got the Holy Spirit indwelling me through faith in Jesus Christ. So, in Jesus' name, leave me alone and go back to the pit."

Exercising my spiritual authority as a Christian indwelt by the Spirit of God always proved my best defense. If particularly intense oppression came, lasting for more than one day, fasting and prayer for God's deliverance was a sure remedy.

On several occasions, Satan sent men to me in an attempt to discredit my ministry of sexual redemption for the homosexual. One such man, a young seminarian, made an appointment to see me. I will call him Bill. At our first meeting I asked him, "Bill, why have you come here?"

Quite frankly he told me, "My spiritual director suggested I come and talk to you about healing for homosexuality. But I don't think this is necessary since I don't think homosexuality is incom-patible with the Bible or Christianity."

"This ministry is for persons who want help. But if you would like to attend our group meeting this Thursday night, you're wel-come to come," I replied.

This first meeting with Bill was rather short. It seemed to me that he had come only to appease his spiritual director. For that reason I did not pray a healing prayer for Bill since this would have violated his will. Bill attended several of our weekly meet-ings and then stopped coming.

The negative spiritual results from my allowing Bill to attend our group meetings were not apparent to me until many years later. By this time, Bill was an ordained minister in his denomination. Another minister from his denomination relayed to me that Bill was now discrediting my ministry. Bill's account of our meeting was, "Years ago I went to Mario Bergner's ministry, but I did not receive any healing." What Bill failed to tell others is that he did not want healing from homosexuality when he came to see me nor did I minister to him.

On another occasion, a man made an appointment to see me under the guise of wanting help. Actually he came to try to seduce me. I will call him Steve. When he came into my office, the Holy Spirit convicted him. He repented of his sin and joined my Living Waters program. After his healing was underway, Steve confessed he had come to me to try to discredit the ministry.

The difference between these two men determined the course of each life. One was humble; the other full of pride. Steve was open to the conviction of the Holy Spirit and repented of his sin. Bill was locked into a proud theological mind-set that rationalized his sin and closed off his soul from God's healing power.

7

The Hatred of Woman

Come, you spirits
That tend on mortal thoughts, *unsex* me here
And fill me, from the crown to the toe, top-full
Of direst cruelty!

Lady Macbeth in Macbeth,
act 1, sc. 5, lines 41b–44a (italics mine)

Kristin's Story

Kristin grew up in a home in which she daily faced the hatred of women as a fact of life. The youngest of four and the only girl, she had childhood memories of being put in the service of her brothers, watching her brothers eat food she was denied, and wearing out-of-style clothes while her brothers dressed as their peers did. Kristin's mother treated her cruelly and clearly preferred her boys. Kristin's father's eyes were never filled with the loving affirmation a little girl so badly needs from her daddy. Rather, he looked at her with lust.

As a teenager, Kristin tried to numb her deep inner pain through drugs. The severe misogyny—hatred of women—caused her to reject her own femininity. Like Lady Macbeth, Kristin was unsexed. She regularly cut her eyelashes because they were too feminine. She adopted a false masculinity in order to survive in this sick home. Internalizing the misogyny in her home, she began hating her own body. When her sexuality first emerged, she engaged in a fantasy life which included images of destructive acts to her own body.

In her late teens she became convinced she was a male trapped in a female body, a condition commonly called transsexuality. As soon as she could, she moved away from home to a large city and entered into its night life. In the gay bars she found other transsexuals and transvestites—her kind of people. Yet because she never met another female transsexual or transvestite, she feared that she was truly a freak. Feeling alone and deeply depressed, she tried to commit suicide, but the attempt failed.

Later she took a trip out West. On the train ride home she sat in the bar car numbing her pain with alcohol. She describes her feelings at that moment: "I thought that I would simply die unless someone touched me." A man sitting across from her invited her to his cabin. All she wanted was for him to hold her. But he had other plans. Not having the strength to fight him off, she thought to herself, *This is the fate of some people; they are born to be raped and abused.*

Months later after that horrible night on the train, Kristin and a friend stumbled into a Christian meeting at a local YMCA. They heard the gospel message, but as Kristin put it, "I was too much of a 'scab' to become a Christian." Still, she returned to the meeting the next week. During his sermon, the preacher said, "If you don't think you're good enough to be a Christian, consider the Apostle Paul. He was a murderer, and Jesus forgave him!"

At these words the dam broke in Kristin's heart. She identified with Paul's sin, for that night on the train she had become pregnant and had later aborted the child. The love of God and the truth of the cross entered into Kristin's soul. She said yes to Christ and, as she puts it, "I took hold of the true hope that can only be found in Jesus." Her conversion brought to her the foundational healing everyone needs, the initial regeneration of the spirit through the new birth and the restoration of a relationship to God.

God quickly began healing the deep confusion in Kristin's heart. Once in a church, she encountered a man who exemplified to her the masculine identity she still wished she had. About him she said, "I wanted to *be* Matthew, physically, emotionally, and spiritually. I wanted to look like him and speak like him. I wanted the ability to lead worship as he did—I wanted his very life." Realizing the depth of her need, she repented of this covetousness, but she also needed to know that she herself was fearfully and wonderfully created by God.

As she waited for God to complete the healing she so desired, she clung to these words of Jesus, "If you obey my commands, you will remain in my love, just as I have obeyed my Father's commands and remain in his love. I have told you this so that my joy may be in you and that your joy may be complete" (John 15: 10–11).

God also led Kristin to read Leanne Payne's book, *Real Presence*. One passage particularly spoke to her:

> The realized and integrated personality, finding its identity only in God, and no longer seeking it in a role (wife, mother, father, churchwoman), in a career or profession (doctor, lawyer, pastor, artist) or in a class (woman, white-collar worker, black), is no longer shaped or determined by fears of failure or by what others think of it. Its justification is in God alone. This redeemed personality is freed from the superimposition of the sins, mistakes, and foibles of others and of those of its own past; it is freed from the rejections it has experienced, both in its past and in its present. It is truly free; free to love—even its own enemies; free to create—in spite of the fears and hate surrounding it. This personality no longer attempts to relate to others (much less to the Body of Christ) on the basis of expertise of any kind, for it no longer finds its identity in that expertise. Fears, outward pressures, undue domination by others no longer shape its inner life, nor even—over too long a period—the circumstances of its outer life; secure within its inner being, it is enabled to confront and to deal with these things rather than be shaped by them. It has, insofar as its finiteness permits, *willed* to be one with God. Its will one with its Cre-

ator's, it can therefore perfectly collaborate with its Creator. Paradoxically appearing to have lost itself, the personality finds itself for the first time truly creative.[1]

This passage Kristin said, "became my heart's cry, my every prayer and my hope for which to live." She ripped out the page from the book and brought it to several Christian counselors. After reading it, they all told her that the ideas expressed there were "too simple, unrealistic for this life." But Kristin pressed on toward the goal of wholeness and maturity in Christ, convinced these were available to her here and now.

She wrote to Leanne Payne, and Leanne suggested that she contact me. Kristin drove nearly one hundred miles each way to attend a weekly support group I led on sexual wholeness in Christ. Although she rarely said much, she was clearly an open vessel waiting eagerly to receive every healing Jesus had for her. She joined the support group midway through the series and was able to attend only a handful of the meetings before the group finished.

After this, I regretted that I had not reached out to her and gotten to know her better. Since I was planning to give a weekend seminar on healing prayer, I invited Kristin to come to it and lead worship. Though she initially agreed to do this, she later wrote to me declining to come. I was saddened by her letter, not because of the loss of a worship leader, but because I knew the Lord had more healing for Kristin. Though her letter did not require a reply, I quickly wrote back expressing my regrets and encouraging her to come anyway but not lead worship.

Eight months went by, and I was getting ready to use a new format for a support group. Andy Comiskey, respected minister in the area of sexual redemption, was in the final stages of rewriting his *Living Waters Sexual Redemption in Christ Program* and graciously allowed me to use it in my ministry. As I was in the process of carefully screening the candidates for the first group, Kristin reappeared. She now lived nearby and wanted to take part in the new program.

Since I had last seen Kristin, much had happened to her. In the previous group, she had begun to accept her femininity and her body. Now for the first time in her life, she experienced feelings of love rather than hatred toward women. But she realized that her heart was still confused when she found herself "falling in love" with one particular woman. Strange as it may seem, lesbian feelings in Kristin's case were a stage in her healing.

But she knew this was not true love and had no desire to seek out a lesbian relationship. Now the neurotic love for a member of her own sex also needed healing.

At the same time she attended a church led by an extremely domineering man. Kristin described him as "the man on top who called *all* the shots, told everyone else what to do, and let his opinions be known from east to west!" As much as she disliked this man, she was drawn to him. She wanted to be his equal. His other-sex ambivalence only called forth Kristin's other-sex ambivalence. Her feelings for him went from serious hatred to physical attraction. She felt that if she could obtain his love, then maybe he would respect her and listen to her. She saw love here, not as an end but as a doorway to equality. In her conscious mind/heart she never really wanted an intimate relationship with him.

Ever since Kristin had attended my first group, she had been greatly ambivalent toward me. The letter I had sent her advising her to come to my seminar whether or not she led worship elicited anger from her. Though she could see that I truly cared for her, in her mind I was just another man giving her advice she did not want. She told me later:

I lost it. Big time! I was enraged and felt nothing but an intense mixture of hate and anger towards you. I literally marched through the house screaming (loudly) crunching and unfolding your letter until it turned to cloth. I was drowning in anger to the point where I couldn't sleep, and I was left massively disturbed for an entire week. In my rational mind I knew you meant only good for me, but I could only feel anger. After one week I finally got on my face and cried my heart out to God. He managed somehow to shine His love into my twisted hardened heart and there revealed my frightening sin.

A synopsis version of this prayer went something like this: "You say in Your Word, God, that You give only good gifts, but You have given me a snake. You have given me a snake for a father, and I hate You for this. I hate this snake, and I hate You. I hate You. I never, ever want to get married because I know You only have a snake for me. No thank You. I don't want any of this."

After spitting out all my anger and finally coming to the end of myself, God said this to me, "Kristin, I give only good gifts, and I didn't give you a snake [for a father] but rather a man who has been fearfully and wonderfully made in my image. I've called him to love Me and serve Me. I've called him to love and affirm you. Yet in his free will he has chosen to serve himself and to follow the cravings of his own heart rather than to seek Me. He has sinned against Me and against you. I call you now to see the real person I've created. I call you now to forgive him and trust Me."

Kristin's ambivalence toward me revealed to her the need to forgive her father. But even after she did this, her struggle with other-sex ambivalence was not over. For the twenty weeks the Living Waters program lasted, I remained the main object of Kristin's angry projections. She fervently disagreed with me in some of the group discussions, but I knew she was not conscious that she was venting her other-sex ambivalence. However, I did make mistakes in dealing with her, for which I later asked forgiveness. Some of her anger at me was warranted, but not all of it.

Kristin and all the participants experienced incredible growth during the time we were together in the Living Waters program. Andy Comiskey's skill at applying theological truths with psychological insight, all the while keeping the gospel in the forefront, is remarkable. Combined with the equipping I had from working alongside Leanne Payne and Pastoral Care Ministries, the program bore life-changing fruit in all our lives. Our times of prayer were moments when heaven and earth met, and the Holy Spirit came to heal God's people. Kristin's healing was such a time.

The Prayer for Kristin

We began the prayer by invoking the name of Jesus and asked the Holy Spirit to come and heal Kristin's mind and heart. Nothing seemed to be happening, so we waited silently on the Holy Spirit, knowing God was at work. After several minutes I asked Kristin if God was showing her anything. "All I see is this picture of myself in the sixth grade. All my hair is chopped off and I look like a boy," she said.

I knew the Lord wanted to resymbolize Kristin's heart the minute she said that. This picture was the symbol Kristin's heart held to define herself as a person. I asked Kristin if she could pull that image of herself out of her mind and give it to Jesus. As she did, she buckled over in pain and began crying with great, tearful sobs.

As we continued in prayer, God revealed that Kristin had been rejected at conception. We simply invoked the presence of Jesus into the moment she was conceived and asked Him to heal the rejection of the infant girl inside her mother's womb. I read Psalm 139:13–16:

> For you created my inmost being;
> you knit me together in my mother's womb.
> I praise you because I am fearfully and wonderfully made;
> your works are wonderful, I know that full well.
> My frame was not hidden from you when I was made in the secret
>   place.
> When I was woven together in the depths of the earth,
> your eyes saw my unformed body.
> All the days ordained for me were written in your book before one
>   of them came to be.

Together as a group, we prayed Kristin through the nine months of fear she experienced while in the womb and the trauma of being born into a world that rejected her. We comforted the little girl inside Kristin by assuring her of God's presence there with her in those first months of life.

Then a memory of her mother's emotional abuse and hatred of her came up. At our urging, Kristin forgave her mother and became free from the sins of her mother against her. Now Kristin's need to receive mother-love became apparent. We simply held her tightly as the Lord did this incredible work of healing and meeting the deficit of love left unmet by a sick mother.

The following is Kristin's account of what followed next:

> The Lord took me to a time in my life where I was extremely frightened (age three). Here I was given the picture of myself and my father in the bathroom where he tried to molest me. I had always feared that this had happened, but could never remember it consciously until we prayed. I could only remember sitting on the toilet for long periods of time (especially at night) just crying.
>
> My bedroom was known to me as the black hole of nightmares where thick black turtle spiders and crazy men with knives lived—the bathroom seemed much safer. In reality when this [the attempted molestation] happened, my reaction was loud and violent. My screaming (I knew at the time) would awaken my mother who was much stronger in my eyes than my father. Just her voice demanded action—which it did that night—and without leaving her bedroom she was able to bring everything to an immediate halt. I ran out of the bathroom, but I'm not sure where to.
>
> After I described this picture to you, you asked me to remain in the room with my father, and then you asked if there was anyone else in the room. I could only see my three brothers standing behind my father facing his back. You then asked me to see Jesus in the room.
>
> At first I couldn't see Jesus at all in the room, and I was filled with fear. I wanted only to get out of the room, but it was so large I couldn't see any door or windows to try to escape. In the moment of my horror, I stepped back realizing there were only men in my vision, a man holding me and [now] men all around me praying. There was absolutely no way out. I had to face them all, especially my father.
>
> Through your constant prayers I was finally able to see Jesus in the room. He came over and picked me off the floor and held me in His arms, and I began growing up. I grew up to the point where I was *equal* in height to my father, and I was able to look him right in the eyes and speak my heart to him.

It is important to note here that what Kristin saw was no longer the actual memory, but a symbolic representation of the healing taking place. Kristin in reality is just over five feet tall, and so to grow to the same height as her father was to symbolically stand up to him and truthfully face him with his sins against her.

> Out poured the fear, the pain, and the deep resentment of being treated like a sexual object. Out came the rage and bitterness I felt at being locked into a twisted sense of being. Out came the hideous disguise as a man that could never quite assure me the protection I needed from him and other men.
>
> I grieved for what seemed to be a very long time, and then you asked me to see him with the eyes of Jesus. You also reminded me constantly that Jesus was there and would always protect me and stand between my father and myself. I needed this constant reminder because it took some time before the fear left.

At this point in the prayer it was necessary to release Kristin from the sins of her father against her. I prayed what could be called an atonement prayer as I confessed to God the sin of misogyny against Kristin by her father and mother, shaping her into a person that God never intended her to be. I asked Jesus to lift from her soul the sin of misogyny and to bind it away from her. Then I asked Jesus to enter into all the areas where Kristin had been shaped by her father's sin against her and to loose her from the negative effects of this sin. I prayed specifically for the light of Jesus to illuminate any areas of her being that felt dirty and defiled by her father's sin. Then, washing her with holy water, I prayed for God to purge these places clean with His holiness. I then asked Jesus to give Kristin divine objectivity about her father and to help her see him as the needy, unredeemed sinner he was.

> When I could finally see my father rightly through the eyes of Jesus, I went on to forgive him and with each word, the fear within me lifted.

At this point in the prayer it became clear that her father's and mother's misogyny had murdered her true feminine identity. Remembering the words of Jesus to Jairus's daughter, I prayed these directly into the dead little girl inside Kristin, "Little girl, I say to you, get up!" (Mark 5:42b). I asked Kristin to look straight up to Jesus and to receive from Him her true self. At this point Kristin's sobs turned to tears of pure joy. Joy itself in the presence of God's Spirit came down from Heaven and lodged in Kristin's soul. Soon those of us praying were all filled with this joy, and shouts of praise, adoration, and thanksgiving to God filled the room.

> After this, Jesus showed me who I really was through His eyes—a beautifully made woman, created in His image and lovely in His sight. (The original picture I had of myself at the beginning of our prayer time was of a very sober, sad-looking child with short, chopped hair. [Now] the picture I had was of a strong beautiful woman, full of joy with curly, long hair.) I was finally free—praise the Lord.

Misogyny

Misogynistic tendencies in men usually appear in forms more subtle than the abusive behavior in Kristin's case or in wife-beating or rape. The subtleties are harder to recognize, but they include such things as:

Pretending to value a woman's input in conversations, but quickly disregarding her comments once made.

Blaming women (as my father blamed my mother).

Resenting woman when she looks to man for help. Seeing her as sickly and helpless.

Always expecting woman to give to man rather than vice versa. This is sometimes cleverly camouflaged in Christian circles where the doctrine on the submission of wives to husbands is emphasized outside its Biblical context of the submission of all believers to each other (Ephesians 5:21).

Locker-room talk between men who refer to their wives in derogatory ways with comments such as "Yah, I let her live in the same house with me," "I feed her, don't I?" "I suppose God could speak through a woman; He spoke through Balaam's donkey," "Once you put a bag over a woman's head, they're all alike." (I regret to be so specific here, but I know that some men reading this book will recognize their own words.)

An inability to thank woman when she has blessed him, taught him something, or given to him in some way.

An inability to receive from woman lest he be indebted to her.

The constant and subtle criticism of one's wife in private while doing the opposite in public.

Most of the misogynistic behavior that so wounds women comes not from homosexual men, but from broken heterosexual men with whom they are in relationship. Dr. Margaret J. Rinck in her fine book, *Christian Men Who Hate Women*, accurately describes much of the pathology behind the man who struggles with misogyny. She points out that such a man's relationships to women will be marked by his ambivalent need to control her while keeping her at a distance.

> In one way, the misogynist builds walls around himself to keep the woman away, fearing that if she gets too close, she'll notice his shame. His bullying has a two-sided purpose; it serves to control her and keep her from abandoning him, but also keeps her at arm's length emotionally. In one way, he comes across as the self-made man, independent, self-assured, confident, needing no one. Yet he is so insecure, so unsure of himself, so unable to separate from her that he sees her, totally and only, as an extension of himself.[2]

Some Christian men with unacknowledged misogynistic tendencies band together into fellowship groups exclusively for men. Those who gravitate to such groups are inevitably looking for affirmation in their masculine identity. Their desire to bond with other Christian men in a healthy way is right. Unfortunately, these groups all too often become a playground for men to exercise their insecurities. They play games, attempting to affirm their masculinity by assuming a role, rather than by identification with Christ. The unique characteristics of some of these groups only express their brokenness.

These men often have grandiose views of themselves, vainly thinking that they are on the cutting edge of Christianity. They are at the mercy of the masculine in isolation from the feminine, which results in a raw drive toward power in the male. The tyrants of this world—Hitler, Mussolini, Stalin, Jim Jones, Saddam Hussein—are always males separated from the civilizing effects of the true feminine.

This drive toward power manifests as they confuse control for leadership. Remember, control is a primary need in the heart of men with misogynistic tendencies. They do not model to the world servant-leadership, as the Scriptures teach (though they may certainly talk about servant-leadership). Rather they are quick to set up an authority structure by which they control those below themselves. One might imagine this structure as a pagan ziggurat temple, which was a steplike pyramid. On the bottom level are all the women in Christendom who are excluded from such groups. One step above them are peon men. Over them are other men, until finally at the top is one man, or a group of men lording it over those below them.

> You know that the rulers of the Gentiles lord it over them, and their high officials exercise authority over them. Not so with you. Instead, whoever wants to become great among you must be your servant, and whoever wants to be first must be your slave. (Matthew 20:25–27)

Most men who submit to such structures never fully exercise their God-given gifts and talents. Only the small group of men at the top are acknowledged to have insight, wisdom, and true giftings. One pastor, a graduate from one of our finest seminaries, who finally left a church run by such a group told me, "I spent ten years sitting on seminary education waiting to be released into leadership, when in reality those above me had no intention of utilizing my gifts and training, lest they lose their control or place of authority."

People who break out of these controlling groups are sometimes accused of having a "disobedient and rebellious spirit." Christian women in leadership who exercise their God-given gifts are criticized by such groups and become prime targets of misogynistic projections. When women insist on using their gifts in obedience to God, these misogynistic men consider them manipulative and controlling or accuse them of having a "Jezebel spirit."

A major negative characteristic of these exclusively male "fellowship groups" is their ability to protect each other when confronted about their problems (sins) and their ability to deflect blame onto others. They have their counterpart in the seedy side of corporate America in the "good-old-boy" network. This age-old alliance of unhealed and needy men exists to maintain power and to cover up each others' shady dealings so that they might remain in power.

Attaining and maintaining the affirmation and acceptance from the other men in the group becomes all-important. Consequently, the wives of men in such groups occupy a less prominent place in their lives. The horrifying outcome is a homocentricity parallel to modern homosexuality and parallel to what St. Paul found in Corinth, men obsessed with relating amiss to men in lieu of relating aright to women.

When man cannot relate to woman in all her giftedness, he pervertedly turns to his own sex in areas where he deems woman unfit. Donald Bloesch in *Is the Bible Sexist?* tells how a low view of woman in the Greco-Roman culture of St. Paul's day resulted in older men seeking intellectual companionship not with their wives but with younger men.

> Among the Greeks men and women did not eat together or even share the same sleeping quarters. Men spent most of their time outside the house, where the wife was confined. Intellectual conversations between husband and wife were discouraged, and many husbands sought out the company of brilliant young men for this purpose.[3]

These "brilliant young men" often became the effeminate partners in pederastic relationships, so common in ancient Greek society. Historically, a devaluation of woman parallels the acceptance of pederasty, homosexuality, and prostitution in a society. The word misogyny itself even comes from the Greek. When we find homosexuality, pederasty, misogyny, we see a society that has begun to disintegrate. Dr. Richard Lovelace in his book *Homo-*

sexuality and the Church, commenting on Romans 2 says, "The homosexuality of any given individual is not the direct punishment of his or her idolatry, but is a product of the damaged social fabric in a society of idolators."[4]

J. B. Skemp in his book, *The Greeks and the Gospels* shows the link between homosexuality, prostitution, and pederasty as they appear as major themes in the literature of ancient Greece. "Homosexual poems are more frequent from Alexandrian times on, and in Attic comedy it is the courtesan who is the constant figure; though there are no squeamishes, at any rate in Aristophanes, about mentioning attachments of men to young handsome boys."[5]

At the heart of the pagan religions of the Near East was the polarized image of woman as either virgin or whore. Both temple prostitutes and temple virgins were central to the idolatrous worship of ancient Greece. The Egyptian cult goddess Isis, who is identified with many of the goddess religions of the Mediterranean, was a mother, a wife, and a whore. Feminist theologians are quick to value goddess religions as superior to the Judeo-Christian religion of Yahweh the Heavenly Father and Jesus His Son. Positively interpreting this view of the goddess as both mother and whore, one feminist scholar states that as a result, "Respectable women as well as prostitutes could identify with her."[6] Yet this view of woman has only devalued her throughout history. What feminist theologians fail to see is that "the revolutionary nature of Judaism's [prohibition against] all forms of nonmarital sex"[7] redeemed woman from her sexually devalued state.

When Paul warns the Corinthians, "Be not deceived: neither fornicators, nor idolaters, nor adulterers, nor effeminate, nor abusers of themselves with mankind [homosexuals, in other versions] . . . shall inherit the kingdom of God" (1 Corinthians 6:9–10b KJV), he is including here the perverted relationships between young men and older men resulting from the inability of Corinthian men to relate to their wives as persons with minds. However, Paul's words here must also be interpreted as an outright denunciation of homosexuality in general, not exclusively pederasty.

Paul, by contrast, encouraged the wife to ask questions and the husband to discuss spiritual matters with her (1 Corinthians 14:35). He pointed out that if one member is deficient, the whole body suffers (1 Corinthians 12:24–26). He rejected the segregation of the sexes both in the home and at worship (cf. 1 Corinthians 11:11). Moreover, he affirmed the full equality of sexual rights in marriage, insisting that each partner meet the erotic needs of the other (1 Corinthians 7:3–5).

The Magna Carta of Christian liberty is Galatians 3:28—"There is neither Jew nor Greek, slave nor free, male nor female, for you are all one in Christ Jesus." Paul was insistent that in Christ there is a basic equality, that men and women are equal heirs to salvation.[8]

Christ broke into a pagan world that readily accepted the polarized view of woman as virgin and whore. When woman is viewed as a virgin, she is a "holy shrine" who ought not to be touched lest she be profaned by man's unworthy hand. In this view she is high and lifted up, more of a holy image than a person. When viewed as a whore, woman is unclean and ought not to be touched lest man profane himself by contact with her. In this view she is more of an object to be used for man's carnal, unholy passions. By coming into the world through the womb of a virgin and by extending His redemptive hand to prostitutes, Jesus delivered woman from these two untouchable states. He related to women as the flesh-and-blood people that they are and wrought their salvation in the same way He did men—the cross.

The Virgin/Whore Complex

In the late 1980s a national television preacher displayed for all the world a prime example of the virgin/whore complex. He was a powerful evangelist. Watching his crusades on television, I heard him preach the simple message of the gospel and rejoiced as hundreds and thousands responded to his invitation to enter into the new birth in Christ.

On his daily television program he was known for his rhetoric against sexual sin, and he frequently invited guests who spoke out rather indiscriminately against the healing ministries of many reputable Christians. Viewers often saw him standing with a Bible in one hand and pointing to an illustration on a chalkboard with the other. Seated at a table below him was a panel of Bible teachers along with the evangelist's wife. As the men discussed Biblical truths, the evangelist's wife would remain silent. She would sit there looking up to her husband while he taught.

On one occasion during a discussion time after a teaching, the evangelist's wife made a statement. She had a good mind, and her contribution to the discussion was rather profound. The evangelist, standing there and looking down at her in her chair, thanked his wife for her comment and quickly picked up the discussion—completely disregarding what she had said. He obviously did not value the good of reason within her (perhaps it did not fit into his image of the ideal Christian wife).

Shortly after that program, this evangelist was exposed for leading a double life. He had for years solicited the services of a prostitute. He quickly repented publicly of his sin and asked his wife's forgiveness.

As I followed the story in the media, I thought that the statements this evangelist made about his wife sounded similar to Romeo's idealized view of Juliet in Shakespeare's play. She was the "ideal wife" and God had "never given a man a better wife." She was high and lifted up, untouchable, a holy shrine, not a person.

The flip side of this holy image of woman was a view of woman as a whore. It was with a prostitute that he sought to fulfill his sexual desires. My heart ached for him as he remorsefully admitted that his compulsion to visit prostitutes had plagued him since he was a youth.

This man's problem rested not merely in his sinful behavior with the prostitute as much as in the sinful condition of his heart holding its polarized images of woman. "For out of the heart come evil thoughts, murder, adultery, sexual immorality, theft, false testimony, slander" (Matthew 15:19). The evangelist presented a classic example of the virgin/whore complex, one aspect of the symbolic confusion behind other-sex ambivalence and misogyny.

It was obvious how the fallen condition of his heart had shaped his theology. His extreme teachings on the submission of wives to husbands and his outright rejection of the more feminine ministries within Christendom (such as healing of the soul) were all symptomatic of his flight from the feminine. His repression of the feminine in himself and in others was a feeble attempt to control the distorted views of woman that propelled him into sinful behavior.

Man, with his fallen view of woman, keeps the prostitution business afloat. If prostitution is the world's oldest profession, then other-sex ambivalence is the world's oldest neurosis.

The healing he needed, and to date still needs, was the very same healing I received—to come to see woman aright, to be healed of other-sex ambivalence and misogyny. Seemingly his theology stressed the need for the new birth to the point of ignoring the Christian's need for ongoing sanctification. His view of conversion seemed to imply that the full redemptive work of the cross happens at the moment of the new birth. Consequently, there was no place in his theology for the Christian suffering with a life-controlling sexual problem. When his denomination rightly insisted he get counseling, he flatly refused. He was caught a second time with a prostitute later.

Freedom from Misogyny

Misogyny is often a root sin at the base of many of the sexual problems people experience. Not only is it related to homosexuality in the male, it is also related to lesbianism and perversions of heterosexuality. It causes endless problems in relations between men and women. The other-sex ambivalence issuing from misogyny hinders the work of the Kingdom of God as we try to collaborate in the mission Christ gave us.

Confessing the sin of misogyny is often key to helping men come free. It was for me. For the man struggling with homosexuality, recognition and repentance of this sin often becomes the first step to entering into his healthy heterosexual identity. For the man with other-sex ambivalence without homosexual neurosis, confession often brings the breakthrough that allows him to enter into trusting and holy relationships with women.

I often pray the following prayer with men in both private and in public meetings to help them break through the sin of misogyny.

> Lord Jesus, I thank You for creating woman and man to be together the image of God. I have not rejoiced nor celebrated woman as fearfully and wonderfully made. I confess this as a sin.
>
> I acknowledge before You, Lord Jesus, that I came into this world through woman's womb. Her body was once the life-source of my body and through her You, O God, gave me my natural life. And through the womb of a virgin all mankind was blessed by the life and ministry of Jesus our Lord and Savior. I realize now that I can never repay woman for the many ways she has been used by You to bless me and all men.
>
> Show me now, Lord, those women I have sinned against. (Wait here in God's presence for a moment for Him to reveal to you any sin in your heart toward any woman.)
>
> I do confess that/these sin(s) up to You. I confess the sin of misogyny. I renounce it in Jesus' name and turn from it. Please forgive me, Jesus, for this sin. (Be sure to wait in God's presence to fully receive His healing forgiveness.)
>
> I ask You now, Lord Jesus, for the grace to love and bless woman as Christ loved and blessed the church, His bride. Show me, Lord, how to give to woman, to bless her, and express my gratitude for her. Free me to unconditionally love her, expecting nothing in return but Your voice telling me, "Well done, good and faithful servant."

It is not unusual to have to ask a woman to pray this prayer too. Girls raised in misogynistic homes grow up to be misogynists. As Christians they will often wholeheartedly embrace distorted teachings of submission of wives to husbands outside the context of mutual submission (Ephesians 5:21).

Some of the subtle ways in which misogyny appears in women include:

> Valuing men's opinions on certain subjects above women's, regardless of whether or not the man has any expertise in that subject.

Despising weak women (often their mothers were weak in the presence of their misogynistic fathers).

Competing with men and even imitating masculine traits in an attempt to compete with greater success.

Preferring their sons over their daughters.

Blaming and/or scapegoating their mothers for problems in the home that ought to be shared with or completely owned by the father.

Needing to be heard and understood by men, but lacking the same need to be heard and understood by women.

Wishing unconsciously (or consciously) that they were men.

For some women, like Kristin, the desire to be a male often surfaces as a full-blown sexual neurosis. These women need to repent of the sin of misogyny and pray the above prayer. They may have to be released from the sin itself, as it has come into their lives through broken relationships with both men and women. This sin may be constricting their souls, shaping them into persons they were never meant to be and repressing their true feminine identity.

For women needing to be released from this sin as it has shaped them, I sometimes pray an atonement prayer:

Come, Holy Spirit, and enter into the depth of my sister's heart. Enter into the dark corners of pain where she has long felt the effects of misogyny. Enter in, Lord Jesus, and begin now to set her free from this sin.

I confess to you, Lord Jesus, the sin of misogyny as it has rested upon this, your daughter. I confess this sin as it has come into her through her father's side of the family and her mother's side. Lift this sin of misogyny off of her soul, Lord Jesus, and bind it far away from her.

Loose her from the negative effects of that sin—any way in which she has despised her own sex, wished she were a male, or simply become a nonperson as a result of this sin. From any way in which this hatred of woman has lodged inside her body and has even caused physical ailments, deliver her now, Lord Jesus, and heal her body.

I ask you, Lord Jesus, to come and bless the true woman in her. Affirm her in her true feminine identity. Fill her with Your love.

These healings can be dramatic, and it is best to pray this type of prayer with several skilled prayer ministers of both sexes. It is especially healing for the suffering one to hear a man pray the atonement prayer confessing the sin of misogyny against her. However, during this time another woman should hold her. If a man holds her, she may shrink back from his touch, as it may have been through the wrong touch of a man that she first encountered this sin. Also when praying for the healing of the feminine toward the end of the prayer, the touch of a whole woman is a perfect sacramental means by which God pours His healing into her. After this, a man may ask the woman for permission to appropriately touch her and then pray a blessing over her as his sister in the Lord.

A Real Woman

Kristin's life continues to show the fruit of prayers such as these. In the months that followed the breakthrough in prayer for her, her femininity blossomed. Many of the men who had been in the Living Waters program attended the same church as Kristin and I. We were all amazed as we watched her, even embarrassing her a bit by all the attention. In hindsight I realize that many of the men saw a real woman for the first time in Kristin.

She later became involved romantically with a young man, a Christian, and this constellated more of her other-sex ambivalence. But she never embraced these confused feelings as truth, nor did she project them onto the young man. Rather she looked straight up to Jesus and brought into His healing presence every confused thought and emotion that welled up from within her. There before her Lord, and with the love and counsel of other trusted Christians, she continued to become the woman God created her to be.

Love was set in order in Kristin because of her painful honesty with herself and God. Kristin's commitment was not to healing; it was to Jesus. In her healing process and in her pain, she never once exchanged the gospel of self-realization for the gospel of Christ.

If Jesus can heal the Marios and Kristins of this world, He can heal anyone.

> Praise be to the God and Father of our Lord Jesus Christ, the Father of compassion and the God of all comfort, who comforts us in all our troubles, so that we can comfort those in any trouble with the comfort we ourselves have received from God. For just as the sufferings of Christ flow over into our lives, so also through Christ our comfort overflows. (2 Corinthians 1:3–5)

Loving the Other Sex

Then the LORD caused the man to fall into a
deep sleep and took one of his ribs and closed
up the place from which he had removed it, and
made the rib into a woman, and brought her to
the man. "This is it!" Adam exclaimed.

Genesis 2:21–23 (TLB)

Kevin and Cindy's Story

Kevin came to me despairing over the problems he and his wife
Cindy were having in their marriage. As we talked, it soon became
apparent that part of the problem was Kevin's other-sex ambivalence, with his wife Cindy as the main recipient of his projections.
In distress, Kevin shared with me that in public he was kind and
gracious to Cindy, but at home he would annihilate her with his
words. With great sincerity he looked me in the eye and said, "I
love her and I want to stop hurting her."

As we talked further, Kevin shared with me a little about his
childhood home and Cindy's. They had both grown up in dysfunctional families where alcoholism was a problem. They

entered into marriage in their early twenties and had no idea what a normal marriage was.

At the beginning of their marriage, they joined a Christian fellowship that taught a lot about the dynamics between men and women within marriage, the family, and the church. Like many churches, this fellowship mistakenly understood masculinity and femininity primarily as roles (or duties) one undertakes in order to be manly or womanly. They were apt to define women as primarily intuitive (the feminine) and man as primarily rational (the masculine). In desperate need of any understanding about gender identity roles (and normalcy), Kevin and Cindy mistakenly embraced rigid teachings about gender roles as well as extreme teachings on discipleship and the submission of wives to husbands. These teachings on submission of wives only fed into Kevin's unconscious other-sex ambivalence and into his desire to be the only object of Cindy's love.

After I explained other-sex ambivalence to Kevin, we prayed for God to search his heart for any confused and distorted views he held of woman. We also prayed specifically that Kevin would no longer allow his relationship with Cindy to prevent her from looking to Jesus as the primary desire of her heart. As happens so often when couples embrace extreme teaching on submission, he had come between his wife and God. That put him in a position he could never live up to, that of always being right. It also caused loneliness, as he could not look to his wife for help when he needed it. This prayer was the first step in freeing both Kevin and Cindy to become all that Jesus created them to be.

Ten days later I met with Cindy and discussed many of the same issues with her. She was a bright woman and was in touch with her inner pain. She shared with me how she had striven to be the perfect daughter, wife, mother, worker, and friend. Cindy had come to define herself primarily by the roles she played in the lives of other people. These relationships shaped her personal identity. In the language of modern popular psychology, she was "codependent."

In its broadest sense, codependency can be defined as an addiction to people, behaviors, or things. When the codependent is addicted to another person, he or she has become so elaborately enmeshed emotionally with the other person that the sense of self—personal identity—is severely restricted, crowded out by the other person's identity and problems.[1]

Since Cindy and Kevin had moved to Ohio a year earlier, her self-confidence had begun to fade, and she now found herself in depression. Her efforts at finding work in her profession had failed (even volunteer positions were filled). She had not lived in Ohio long enough to establish any deep friendships. Cindy was stripped of all the roles by which she could define herself. She felt like a nonperson.

Growing up with alcoholism, she had adopted a survival role in this dysfunctional family—that of the family hero. She had to make sure everything in the family was fine, often covering the mistakes of others in order to keep the peace. Cindy lived in constant fear of abandonment—a fear common to adult children of alcoholics. Specifically stated, she feared that if her husband found out she was not perfect, he would abandon her. Author Janet G. Woititz writes:

> The constant fear, however, is that the person you love will not be there for you tomorrow. In an attempt to guard against losing your beloved, you idealize the relationship, and idealize your role in the relationship. Your safeguard against being abandoned is to try hard to be perfect, and serve all the other person's needs.[2]

When Cindy encountered the extreme teachings on the submission of wives to husbands, which included hearing her calling from God through Kevin, it only fed into her codependent pattern of relating. It could be said that Cindy mistakenly embraced God's proclamation to Eve, "Your desire will be for your husband, and he will rule over you" (Genesis 3:16), as a command, rather than seeing it as a curse of the Fall, from which Jesus died to redeem her.

The prayer for Cindy's healing was a simple one, that of setting her eyes on Jesus and making Him the primary source of her desire. I also encouraged Cindy to join a reputable Christian Adult Children of Alcoholics (ACOA) support group so that she could begin to deal with the issues common to ACOAs. After her spiritual needs were attended to, she needed the good of psychological insight to help her walk out her healing. Once she began to face the effects of growing up in a dysfunctional home, issues would come up requiring the support of others with similar backgrounds.

I also encouraged Kevin to attend such a group, but he was still in denial about the alcohol problem in his childhood home. Kevin had sincerely sought God for his healing for quite some time and was rather impatient with the thought that some process might be involved. I prayed for God to give him patience with himself and asked the Lord to slowly bring him out of denial regarding his dysfunctional family.

Meanwhile, God was graciously working in Cindy's life, affirming her identity in Him and healing her of codependency in the process. I soon received this letter from her glorifying our Lord.

Dear Mario,
    I am rejoicing in who I am becoming. The day after we prayed, the Lord revealed to me that I had my husband as an idol, marriage as an idol, and family as an idol. I had taken these God-given gifts and made them idols. I have renounced them as idols and have asked for God's forgiveness.
    Your prayer for centeredness in Christ was the beginning for me of seeing myself as separate from my husband, my children, and from my mother. I need to learn how to walk in that centeredness in Jesus on a daily basis.
    God continues to show me how I have related to others in the past, that I am a nonperson unless I am relating to someone. It is how I coped growing up in an alcoholic home. No one at home paid attention to me. So I became involved in lots of activities with people. I had never been affirmed in who I am as an individual person, only in relation to someone else.
    The Lord has revealed this since I have moved here. No friends, no job—attempts to make friends, and even volunteer work have failed. It's like He had to remove everything so I could meet Him face to face. I desire to be free so much, and I know that God has brought me so far that He will complete the work in me. It's exciting, but also scary, in that I am afraid of the hurt that might be in there.

When you prayed and put the cross next to my heart, something profound happened. I felt Jesus drawing the pain out of my being. I had always found it hard to personalize Jesus taking my sin and hurt into His body at the cross. It was as if it was for everyone, except me. The picture in my mind was of Jesus on the cross up on a hill, and I was at the bottom of the hill throwing my sins, and hurts, and cares up to Him. Only they would always fall back down on me—like they had never quite made it to the cross. With the cross held so close to my heart, the pain and hurt went right into Jesus—no room to fall back down. Thank you, Jesus, for creative ways of praying.

Sometimes when someone has trouble receiving from Jesus, I will take a crucifix and have the person hold it to his or her heart. The symbolic representation of Jesus on the cross immediately spoke to Cindy's heart and bypassed her painful thinking about her sins falling back onto herself.

I know that Jesus is saying, "Dear one, come forth, little girl, come forth." And all that is affecting my family will be taken care of.

When I left your apartment, I was thankful [for the first time] that I had moved here.

Thank you, Cindy

After this initial spiritual healing of receiving (really for the first time) the forgiveness of sins, Cindy came to a Pastoral Care Ministries School and received even more insight and personal healing. She then joined an ACOA group, where she walked out her healing and properly dealt with the issues unique to growing up in an alcoholic home.

This was not an easy trek for Cindy or for Kevin, for it meant dealing with the dysfunctional ways of relating they had carried into their marriage. Feelings they were forced to repress in their childhood homes were now given permission to surface. Both Kevin and Cindy were called to own for themselves the negative emotions related to their past and to cease projecting those emotions onto each other.

However, because both Kevin and Cindy were in a loving community of Christian believers, and because their eyes were firmly

set on Jesus—no longer idolatrously bent toward each other—
they progressed through the rest of their healing.

Other-Sex Ambivalence

Ambivalence toward the other sex is one of the greatest barriers preventing men and women from relating rightly to one
another. Though both women and men may experience ambivalence toward the other sex, women are more often the object of
ambivalence by both sexes. This may be related to a developmental step during infancy when all children experience ambivalence toward mother. If we have not successfully passed through
this developmental stage, our unresolved ambivalence toward
mother may generalize toward all women. As adults, we may then
unconsciously project onto women unhealed issues (such as
rejections) related to mother.

Other-sex ambivalence is often as important a factor in the
homosexual neurosis as same-sex ambivalence. For the man
overcoming homosexuality, as I was, failure to work fully through
his ambivalence toward woman means failure to come fully into
his true heterosexual identity. Because the person from a homosexual background has grown up with deficits of same-sex love,
it is not uncommon for him to become centered in on his same-
sex love needs, what might be called homocentricity. Homosexuality could be seen as the failure to rightly see the other sex due
to an unhealthy preoccupation with the same sex. In order to face
the otherliness of the other sex, one must feel secure with the
same sex.

For the heterosexual man, other-sex ambivalence may manifest as a fear of commitment to woman. He is incapable of relating to a woman long enough or deeply enough to allow true love
to awaken. Additionally, he may underestimate woman as a
human being and, like the homosexual, be caught in homocentricity. He may have an obsession to please other men or be overly
concerned with "what the boys" think of him. If married, he may
be unfaithful to his wife. If a Christian, he may suppress her under
an extreme requirement of submission to him. On the far end
of the spectrum, other-sex ambivalence in men is related to

misogyny, the hatred of woman. Misogyny is the root issue in the abuse of women via pornography and rape.

Other-sex ambivalence usually comes from the unhealed hurts, rejections, fears, and confusion about the other sex from our past. As adults we unknowingly project these unhealed issues onto the other sex. Because of the unconscious nature of these projections, we fail to recognize the ambivalence when it occurs.

As men, we are only aware of our irrational irritations with certain women, fear of some women, and overwhelming sexual temptation toward some. These irritations, fears, and sexual temptations really stem from psychological projections. At times one woman in our life is the primary recipient of these projections. She may be our mother, wife, daughter, sister, girlfriend, or colleague. (From here on when I refer to other-sex ambivalence, I am referring to men's ambivalence toward women.)

The woman who is the object of our ambivalence may sense something is wrong but fail to realize that the problem is not with her. She may frantically search her own heart for a fault that is not there. She may react to our ambivalence by feeling angry when we blame her for something she has not done. Then having a wrong understanding of anger, she might come to us and confess her anger (which under the circumstances is warranted). This only reinforces our ambivalent feelings toward her. We may now blame her for the problem, thinking to ourselves, *She has a lot of unresolved anger.* Actually the problem is within our own hearts. When this is the case, we are like the man in the Gospel parable, picking out splinters in another's eye while having a plank lodged in our own.

The blaming of woman is a common expression of man's ambivalence toward her. In the Bible in one of the first interactions between fallen man and fallen woman, he puts blame on her. After God asks the man if he ate the fruit from the tree, Adam says to God, "The woman you put here with me—she gave me some fruit from the tree and I ate it" (Genesis 3:12). Rather than taking responsibility for his own actions, Adam points the finger to Eve before finally admitting, "I ate it."

Leaving Mother Behind

Our hearts often hold distorted and confused images of the other sex. These images are the containers of all the negative and sinful attitudes we have toward that sex. Truly broken images, they result from living in a fallen world—a world where families are often dysfunctional, where the Hollywood blonde is the societal ideal of woman, and where the church has often failed to see woman rightly.

In our fallen condition, we may also have distorted images of the other sex as a result of our sinful reactions to their sins against us. Often these are reactions to our mothers. Until such reactions are dealt with, we, as men, may fail to leave mother behind—thereby failing to find the freedom to be rightly united to woman and become one flesh with her. "A man will leave his father and mother and be united to his wife, and they will become one flesh" (Genesis 2:24). Walter Trobisch writes:

> The Bible is very down to earth and sober. It says, "A man leaves his father and mother." Leaving is the price of happiness. There must be a clean and clear cut. Just as a newborn baby cannot grow up unless the umbilical cord is cut.[3]

The man who has not left mother behind cannot give to another woman, cannot serve that woman, nor love her. In the immature position, such a man will relate to woman from a perspective of his own needs. As a result, he will tend to see her as an extension of himself, rather than as other than himself. In the conjugal bed, he may be more aware of the pleasure he is receiving than the pleasure he is giving. In the context of Christian marriage, he may embrace teachings on the submission of wives that require only the wives to continually give to their husbands. By contrast, in the Biblical model man assumes the character of Christ—giving to the wife even unto death.

The Bible does not also command woman to leave her mother and father behind. One reason might be that woman has an easier task at realizing her gender identity. Unlike man, who must separate both his personal and sexual identity from mother, woman needs only to get her personal identity separated from mother. She shares the same sexual identity as mother, whereas the man does not, and he must come to realize this.

Some homosexuality in the male is related to his inability to fully separate his gender identity from mother. In the case of transsexuality and transvestitism in the male, it is more a problem of failing to separate both his gender and sexual identity from mother. In these cases, mother may have been emotionally needy, exceedingly controlling, or even sexually abusive toward her son, resulting in a diseased bond between mother and child. Until this unhealthy bond with mother is recognized and broken, these sons—whether they be homosexuals, transsexuals, or transvestites—cannot mature emotionally enough to realize that their gender identity is different from mother's.

In *The Broken Image*, Leanne Payne writes of the need for the sexually neurotic to find freedom from a diseased bond to mother. In context, the quote below is taken from an account of a woman's healing from lesbianism. However, what Leanne has written is also applicable for men needing to leave mother behind.

> In the prayer for such a one's release, I usually ask them to see Jesus with the eyes of their hearts, to see Him on the cross, there taking into Himself the very pain and bondage they are now struggling with, as well as any unforgiveness or sin within their hearts. I ask them to stretch out their hands to Him and see the pain and darkness flow into His outstretched, nail-riven hands as I pray for the severance of their souls from the domination of their mothers. I often, without interrupting the rhythm of the prayer, softly ask them, "What are you seeing with the eyes of your heart?" And it is wonderful what they see as the darkness flows out of them and into Him. Often I will be seeing the same "picture" as the Holy Spirit leads the way.
>
> Then, and I find this to be a very important step, I ask them to picture their mother. Because the Holy Spirit is in control and healing is so powerfully taking place, they will nearly always have a picture of her that is most revealing, one that will enable them to see her objectively for the first time, one that will better enable them to forgive her. Then I ask them to look and see if there are

any bondages left between them. They will see it and name it. I then ask them, as though they had scissors in their hands, to cut through the bonds they see. The release that comes with this is often nothing short of phenomenal, and there are times when there are definite emotional and even physical reactions to the release. We will have seen these bonds sometimes like thick diseased umbilical cords, other times as threadlike ropes between the souls of the two, etc. When they are cut, we see a symbolic picture, one that is a true one, of the very deliverance that is taking place.[4]

Leaving mother behind is key to facing the world of the other, key to loving woman aright.

Developmental Ambivalence toward Mother

The function of a mother is not exhausted with sheltering, protection and dependence. By the very act of birth she puts us into the world; you might almost say that the first encounter with her involves being pushed away by her. At birth the umbilical cord is severed, and if the mother's love for the child is healthy, a gentle process of severing continues, not only physically but mentally. The mother shows the child that he is not the exclusive recipient of her love. She teaches him to share her affection with others. She turns his gaze away from her. He has to face reality. Only the neurotic mother maintains her child in a state of dependence and fixation; the wise mother knows not only how to bind, but also how to sever. In fact, man is truly capable of loving only if the psychological bond of maternal fixation is disconnected. Only then are we able to face the world and the "other."[5]

When a child comes to realize that he is not the only recipient of mother's time and love, it is common for that child to experience ambivalence toward her. I saw this clearly one day when visiting my sister Karen. I arrived while her son, Alexander, then about ten months old, was taking his afternoon nap. Doting uncle that I am, I happily went into his room to get him the moment he awakened. I picked him up and carried him, still groggy with his eyes full of sleep, into the kitchen. He looked like a cherub with tousled golden curls. Upon seeing Karen, he angrily turned his head away from her.

Laughing, Karen came over to us with open arms and said, "Come on, Alex, come to Mama."

He swung his arm at my sister as if to hit her, turned his face in the other direction, and rested his head on my shoulder.

"Isn't that sweet, Karen. He's happy to see me."

"Don't get your hopes up, Mario," she responded knowingly. "He's mad at me because I had to put him down this morning and get on with my work around the house."

Indeed, this little guy of no more than a year was angry with his mother for "being pushed away" by her. He was now doing the same back in retaliation. Had she not been wise to his infantile tactics, she might have tried to appease him. That would only have taught him that anger is the appropriate response when he is not the sole object of her time and love. Had Karen given in to this little rascal in his behavior, in time he would have acquired an image of woman as nothing more than a westernized geisha, ever waiting to be beckoned into action for her man. Eventually, Alexander might have developed a full-fledged case of other-sex ambivalence.

How many men have unwarranted reactions to a woman who merely says no? Or how many men in a love relationship with a woman are jealous once they realize that they are not the exclusive recipient of her time and love?

Seeing Woman

Man comes to know woman by experiencing her, by close contact with her. In every man resides a beautiful God-given need not only to encounter but also to deeply commune with woman. This is rooted in the fact that before the separation of Eve from Adam, they were together in one body.

> Then the Lord God made a woman from the rib he had taken out of the man, and he brought her to the man. The man said, "This is now bone of my bones and flesh of my flesh; she shall be called 'woman,' for she was taken out of man." (Genesis 2:22–23)

Adam felt the need to become one flesh with Eve because he had once before been one flesh with her. Whether fully aware of it or not, all men by design have the same need to commune with woman, to be reunited with her, to become one with her. About this Walter Trobisch writes:

> This story is the most wonderful and unique description of the reality of love. Why do the sexes long for each other without ceasing? How can it be explained that they are magnetically attracted to each other? The answer is: They are made out of the same piece ... they are parts of a whole and want to restore this whole again, want to complete each other, want to become "one flesh."[6]

I first read of this magnetic attraction between the sexes in Karl Stern's classic book, *The Flight from Woman*. Dr. Stern writes:

> The most famous presentation of this idea is found in Genesis when God created man in His image, "male and female"—before the separation of Eve out of the body of Adam.[7]

At the time I was still being healed of my homosexual neurosis. Upon reading Stern's description of the separation of Eve out of Adam, I felt as if fireworks went off inside my body. I suddenly realized I could only know the fullness of being made in God's image by reuniting with woman. Apart from whether I believed it or not, by God's design, there was a part of me as a man that needed to be with woman. It was only a matter of time before this need for woman fully emerged from its repressed state within me. Actually, this insight alone sparked a sexual interest in woman that I had never had before. For the first time, I believed it possible for me to receive joy and pleasure from sexual union with a woman.

As I practiced the presence of the Lord, more of my true masculine self came forward every day. No longer homocentric (centered on my own sex), I became more outwardly directed, more interested in things outside and other than myself. As a result, I began noticing things I had failed to see before. At first God's creation and His creatures possessed a new beauty for me, the gentle hills of southwestern Ohio and my gray tabby cat, The Little Guy.

A new, pleasant awareness of differences between my male and female students caught my imagination, something I now understand awakens in most people during puberty. As a teacher of voice and speech, I had some expertise in kinesthetics (the study of the body as it moves in space). Differences between a woman's walk and a man's walk or the differences between the way each sits seemed to leap out at me. These were not things I sought to notice. Rather they caught onto me and refused to let go until I paid them proper attention.

One afternoon a female student came to my office for a tutorial in Shakespeare text. After entering my office, she sat in a sturdy chair, and I methodically checked the alignment of her skeletal frame to make sure her body was positioned for optimal breath support and comfort. Then I sat in a chair opposite her and listened as this pretty girl with ginger-colored hair recited the text. Suddenly, my eye caught sight of a particularly beautiful part of her body. For some reason unknown to me, I was transfixed. Captivated and held motionless, I failed to hear a word she was reciting.

Noticing I was not paying attention, she called out to me, "Mario? Mario?"

I sat there with my jaw open trying to respond, but I was so enthralled that my mouth could not form any words. I tried to speak, but the huge lump in my throat allowed only croaking sounds to emerge.

Concerned, Carol cautiously asked me, "Mario, is everything all right?"

Not knowing if everything was all right, I swallowed the lump in my throat and choked out, "Uh, I, uh, don't know."

Thinking about this for a moment and feeling rather foolish for gawking at this student, I sheepishly asked her, "Carol, uh, could you leave?"

"Sure," she replied. Looking at me strangely, she leaped from her chair and bounced out of my office.

As I was sitting in the chair opposite her, the light in my office had fallen upon her face, bringing a beautiful hue to her cheek.

The softness of her skin and its silky pink color illuminated under the light looked like nothing I had ever seen before. It was so different from the way light could have ever fallen on a man's face.

The beauty of that small portion of her face spoke to a place deep within me. A variety of unexplainable feelings ran through my body like a river of delight and joy. The more I looked at her, the more I felt it. I didn't want to stop.

Not knowing what these feelings were, I began to pray after she left and simply asked the Lord, "What was that?!"

Then, as if an angel came into my office carrying Shakespeare's poetry on a silver platter, these words of Romeo when he saw Juliet upon her balcony came to mind:

> See, how she leans her cheek upon her hand!
> O, that I were a glove upon that hand,
> That I might touch that cheek.
>
> *Romeo and Juliet*, act 2, sc. 2, lines 23–25

In touch with my masculinity for the first time and no longer preoccupied with my own sex, I had eyes to see the otherliness of the other sex.

I saw woman.

Upon seeing the woman the Lord God brought to him, Adam joyfully exclaimed: "This is it!" (Genesis 2:23 TLB). So too did my soul exclaim joyfully at seeing woman for the first time. Like Adam, I also recognized a part of myself in her: "This is now bone of my bones and flesh of my flesh; she shall be called 'woman' for she was taken out of man" (Genesis 2:23). The chasm between myself and woman was bridged. Paradoxically, while discovering the otherliness of woman, I was also awakening to the similarities of woman to man. Captivated by Carol's femininity, I also sensed that I shared a common humanity with her. Odd as this may seem, I had never before experienced this ordinary connection between myself and a woman.

The undefinable pleasure aroused within me by seeing woman was so foreign to me that I simply did not know what was happening. In hindsight, I understand that I was experiencing the normal sexual response a man feels toward a woman he finds attractive. Because I only knew sexual arousal in its overwhelming lustful neurotic form, I had no standard for recognizing this new real sexuality emerging from its repressed state within me.

The healthy sexual appetite is soft and subtle, not loud and clanging. Coming from a homosexual background, however, I expected my sexual desire for woman to have the same lustful overwhelming power as my former neurotic sexual attraction to men. I've since talked to many men who have overcome homosexuality. In their healing process they too have discovered this same difference between homosexuality and healthy heterosexuality. Men whose sexual drive toward woman is overwhelming and lustful are manifesting a need for healing in their sexuality. This drive is not a sign of their virility as men.

A Death-Marked Love

The sexual awakening I had while tutoring my student paralleled what most males experience in adolescence. I did not go looking for it; rather it found me, catching me off guard. Though this awakening was natural and real, it needed to mature. Like the first love of adolescence, it was characteristically narcissistic. My feelings for this student were the main focus of this experience, not her as a person.

At first I was a bit embarrassed to be going through puberty at age twenty-five. But it seemed that many of my male colleagues at the university, most of them older than I, were not much more mature sexually. At this point I realized that people in today's society love much like adolescents still in puberty. Members of the me-generation display a narcissism and self-consciousness that make it practically impossible to see anything other than themselves.

Many who read or see the play *Romeo and Juliet* think it is a story of true love. In my estimation it is not. Shakespeare properly titled it *The Tragedy of Romeo and Juliet*.

Most persons in today's fallen and broken world have confused true love with tragic romantic ideas about love. Though I doubt this is why Shakespeare wrote his classic, his text certainly could be interpreted as a statement about tragic immature and narcissistic love.

The play begins with a prologue in sonnet form. Sonnets were a form of love poetry popular during the Elizabethan Age. They were read aloud at gatherings of the court and were the mode of expression for the then-fashionable courtly love.

Shakespeare's sonnets are charged with highly potent language and imagery, with tightly woven relationships between the words. When Shakespeare inserted a sonnet into a play, he sent his audience a message that something important was happening. Several beautiful sonnets appear throughout the play as highlights to key moments.

The sonnet opening *Romeo and Juliet* reveals the entire plot and appropriately describes the love between these two teenagers as "star-crossed" and "death-marked."

> A pair of star-cross'd lovers take their life;
> Whose misadventured piteous overthrows
> Do with their death bury their parents' strife.
> The fearful passage of their death-mark'd love,
>
> Prologue, lines 6–9

We first see Romeo talking with his cousin Benvolio. Romeo is lovesick because his current love, Rosaline, has sworn herself to a chaste life. His cousin advises him to forget her.

Certain that meeting another girl will solve Romeo's problem, Benvolio leads Romeo to a party. When they arrive, all the guests are wearing masks. Romeo first sees Juliet's face from afar, before she puts on her mask. He covers his face with a mask and approaches her. She too now wears a mask. The first fourteen lines they speak to one another form another sonnet.

> Romeo: If I profane with my unworthiest hand
>   This holy shrine, the gentle sin is this:
>   My lips, two blushing pilgrims, ready stand
>   To smooth that rough touch with a tender kiss.
> Juliet: Good pilgrim, you do wrong your hand too much,
>   Which mannerly devotion shows is this:

> For saints have hands that pilgrims' hands do touch,
>   And palm to palm is holy palmer's kiss.
> Romeo: Have not saints lips, and holy palmers too?
> Juliet: Aye, pilgrim, lips that they must use in prayer.
> Romeo: O, then, dear saint, let lips do what hands do;
>   They pray, grant thou, lest faith turn to despair.
> Juliet: Saints do not move, though grant for prayers' sake.
> Romeo: Then move not while my prayer's effect I take.[9]
> [He kisses her.]

Act 1, sc. 5, lines 95–108

Note that neither Juliet nor Romeo are seeing each other directly. They are both looking at masks. It is perfectly frightening how often two people fall in love with the other's social mask (one's appearance) and not with the person behind the mask (the real self). How little immature love has changed in four hundred years. Notice too that in Romeo's first words to Juliet, he describes her as a holy shrine, whom to touch would be to profane. Juliet is no ordinary woman to Romeo.

Act 2 begins with yet another sonnet, part of which reads:

> Now Romeo is beloved, and loves again,
> Alike bewitched by the charm of looks,[10]

Act 2, prologue, lines 5–6

It seems that Romeo, like many in the twentieth century, has fallen for a pretty face.

Under the spell of love, Romeo now climbs over the wall that separates Juliet's courtyard from the street and stares up at her bedroom window. While hiding in the garden, he sees his "love" and speaks the famous lines:

> But, soft! what light through yonder window breaks?
> It is the east, and Juliet is the sun.
> Arise, fair sun, and kill the envious moon,
> Who is already sick and pale with grief,
> That thou her maid art far more fair than she:
> Be not her maid, since she is envious;
> Her vestal livery is but sick and green

And none but fools do wear it; cast it off.
It is my lady, O, it is my love!
O, that she knew she were!
She speaks, yet she says nothing: what of that?
Her eye discourses; I will answer it.
I am too bold, 'tis not to me she speaks:
Two of the fairest stars in all the heaven,
Having some business, do entreat her eyes
To twinkle in their spheres till they return.
What if her eyes were there, they in her head?
The brightness of her cheek would shame those stars,
As daylight doth a lamp; her eyes in heaven
Would through the airy region stream so bright
That birds would sing and think it were not night.
See, how she leans her cheek upon her hand!
O, that I were a glove upon that hand,
That I might touch that cheek.[11]

Act 2, sc. 2, lines 2–25

Earlier at the party, Romeo, under love's spell, was so charmed by Juliet that he saw her as a holy shrine. Now in her courtyard, he sees her as the sun, the moon, the stars in the heavens. This poor guy is so star-crossed, he sees Juliet as everything but the flesh and blood woman she really is. He is not truly in love with the person Juliet as much as he is in love with the way his heart symbolizes her (holy shrine, sun, moon, stars). It could be said that he is in love with the idea of Juliet or the appearance of Juliet. Romeo has confused the appearance of love for the reality of love.

By the end of the courtyard scene, they have vowed to marry each other. As Romeo is leaving, Juliet calls him back. Romeo's reply to Juliet's call warrants special attention.

It is *my soul* that calls upon my name.
How silver-sweet sound lovers' tongues by night,
Like softest music to attending ears![12]

Act 2, sc. 2, lines 164–167 (italics mine)

This is one of the most revealing lines Romeo speaks in the entire play. Juliet also symbolizes Romeo's soul to him. Because the soul is feminine, it is common for man to see in woman some aspect of his soul. In the Scriptures, the soul is symbolized as feminine, hence both men and women are called "the bride of Christ."

The desire Romeo and Juliet have for each other is partially fueled by the fact they belong to families that have been feuding with each other. In our fallenness we perversely desire that which is forbidden to us. Forbidden desire is often a driving force behind passionate adulterous love affairs. Should the adulterous partner divorce his spouse, he quickly finds that the fire dies out of this new "love." At that point he commonly longs for the real love once shared with the spouse left behind. As fallen creatures, we sometimes purposely desire what is denied to us. Once we obtain what we carnally desire, we often feel empty and unfulfilled.

Romeo now asks Friar Laurence to marry them. At first the friar thinks Romeo is still in love with Rosaline. He is shocked to learn that Romeo is now "in love" with Juliet and wants to marry her after knowing her for so short a time. He says:

> Holy Saint Francis, what a change is here!
> Is Rosaline, whom thou didst love so dear,
> So soon forsaken? Young men's love then lies
> Not truly in their hearts, but in their eyes.[13]
>
> Act 2, sc. 3, lines 61–68

But thinking that marriage between these two members of feuding families might bring about reconciliation, the friar agrees to perform the ceremony.

As Romeo and the friar await Juliet's arrival before the secret ceremony takes place, Romeo tells the friar:

> Do thou but close our hands with holy words,
> Then love-devouring death do what he dare;
> It is enough I may but call her mine.[14]
>
> Act 2, sc. 6, lines 6–8

Tragic love is narcissistic; it is self-seeking. Romeo is concerned with possessing Juliet as one might an object. Scripture teaches us that real love is exactly the opposite: "[Love] is not self-seeking . . ." (1 Corinthians 13:5).

Romeo and Juliet are wed, and shortly afterward Romeo's close friend Mercutio dies by the sword of Juliet's cousin Tybalt. Mercutio's last words to Romeo are: "A plague o' both your houses!"

Tragic love also brings destruction to the lives around it. Mercutio's curse on both families conveys the nature of tragic love; it is not blessed.

At this point in the play Paris appears. He is perhaps the only person in this story who approaches true love. The one he loves is Juliet. He has secured the hand of his bride-to-be by going through the proper channel—asking her father. The parents set a wedding date. (Only Romeo, Juliet, Juliet's nurse, and the friar know about the secret marriage.) Juliet is horrified by her father's plans to marry her to Paris. She does not love Paris, and she is already a married woman.

By accident Romeo kills Tybalt in a street fight. Now wanted for murder, he must go into hiding.

Juliet sinks into despair over her approaching wedding and Romeo's fugitive status. Seeking help, she meets with the friar, who devises a plan to save them all. He gives Juliet a potion which, when swallowed, will put her into a sleep so deep that those who find her will think she is dead. Once Juliet is laid in a tomb and left for dead, the friar will bring Romeo to her side. Then everything will be all right.

But tragic love attracts disaster and seems to be empowered by it. Despite two deaths already, the eyes of these two star-crossed lovers remain unopened. Tragic love is secretive. It cannot be shared with others. True love is free to invite others to partake of the joy the lovers share. True love gives; it blesses all who come into its path.

Tragic love is irresponsible; it takes the easy way out. Romeo does not take responsibility for killing Tybalt. Rather he runs away. Juliet does not take responsibility for marrying Romeo. She lies to her father and does not tell him she cannot marry Paris. The easy way out of this mess is to take a "magic potion." When its effect has worn off, everything will be all right.

Tragic love is idolatrous. Romance between man and woman may be so distorted that it becomes almost worship. We may seek to experience in romantic love a consuming sensation. The only other place man dares to seek this all-consuming sensation is in the religious awe experienced in the presence of God. We seek in romantic love a feeling of wholeness. The only other place we dare seek wholeness is in God, in relationship to Jesus. As long as we're "in love," the world is beautiful, filled with color, in a never-ending spring. When we're not "in love," the world is a cold, cloudy February day in Pittsburgh.

Why is it that when Romeo is lovesick at the beginning of the play, he turns to the friar for advice? Why, when their relationship is threatened, does Juliet turn to him as well? It is because the friar is a symbol of the church, the representative of God.

Adam and Eve knew true religious awe before the Fall. Because they were rightly related to God, they were rightly related to each other. They saw each other as they truly were without projecting onto each other their idealized image of the perfect lover. For this reason, they could stand shoulder to shoulder, side by side, naked and not ashamed before God and each other. It was only after the Fall that Adam and Eve felt shame and covered themselves with fig leaves. In doing so, they put up the first masks to cover the real self.

The friar's plan backfires. Because Romeo is in hiding, the friar cannot contact him to inform him that Juliet is not dead, only in a drug-induced sleep. After Juliet is laid in her tomb, Romeo hears of Juliet's "death." Thinking he has lost his love, he goes to an apothecary (Elizabethan drugstore) to buy some poison. Then he goes to Juliet's tomb to kill himself next to his beloved.

To Romeo's surprise, at the tomb he finds Paris, who has come to grieve the loss of Juliet. The two meet and have a duel, in which Romeo kills Paris. Then Romeo opens the tomb and carries Paris's body in with him. After finding Juliet's "dead" body, he kisses her one last time, drinks the poison, and dies.

Romeo does not go to Juliet's tomb to mourn, but to kiss Juliet dramatically for the last time and to take his own life. He does not consider the pain and sorrow he will cause his family and friends by his suicide. Tragic love does not consider the feelings of others.

Paris, on the other hand, goes to Juliet's tomb to mourn her death, to say good-bye. Grief is the proper response to the loss of true love. Though genuine grief often contains elements of despair, and the bereaved one wonders how to go on living, he knows better than to inflict more pain by taking another life. Paris by grieving proves he loved Juliet aright. Romeo doesn't take the time to grieve.

Shortly afterward the friar, old and slow, arrives at Juliet's tomb, only to find both Romeo and Paris dead. The magic potion given to Juliet wears off, and she awakens. The friar tries to convince her to flee as he hears others approaching her tomb. But she will not go and commands the friar to leave. Alone, with the bodies of Paris and Romeo, she gives Romeo one last kiss, takes his dagger, and kills herself.

Juliet (like Romeo) does not think of grieving; she too opts for suicide. In some productions, the dagger Juliet uses on herself is the same one Romeo used to kill Paris—an ironic twist. Paris's love for Juliet is the only love in this entire play that approaches reality. The dagger then becomes a symbol of what tragic love does to true love—it kills it.

The families of Romeo and Juliet arrive along with the Prince of Verona. In despair over the loss of life, the two families reconcile, and the play ends with these words:

> For never was a story of more woe
> Than this of Juliet and her Romeo.[15]

Act 5, sc. 3, lines 309–310

The Idealized Image of Woman

Like Romeo, I too passed through a stage of idealizing woman. After resigning from my teaching job at Wright State University, I moved to Milwaukee for three years. During this time I worked with a Christian theater company where I met "Melanie." Melanie was, and still is I suspect, a larger-than-life woman. Full of energy and very animated, she reminded me of my student who had ignited the first sparks of normal sexuality in me. I "fell in love." Melanie, however, was not in love with me.

After working with her in several plays, my romantic feelings toward her became strong. This might have been all right had she reciprocated. But she even went to the trouble of meeting with me and kindly telling me that she was not interested, which I genuinely appreciated. After that meeting I decided to stop pursuing her. But my heart had other plans. Though I knew rationally that there was no hope of a relationship between us, I continued to have very strong feelings toward her. She even frequently appeared in my dreams.

At the same time, Leanne Payne and I became friends. I shared with Leanne some of my feelings for Melanie, and she was delighted—until I told her about the dreams I was having in which both she and Melanie appeared. From the content of these dreams, she realized that both Melanie and herself were highly idealized figures for me. I was not prepared to understand what all this meant at that time, but from Leanne's counsel, I realized that in my dreams both Melanie and Leanne symbolized my own feminine and that I was to take my dreams figuratively and not literally. In other words, I was not literally dreaming about Melanie and Leanne; I was dreaming about the part of myself that they represented.

After sharing some rather perplexing dreams about Melanie with Leanne, Leanne told me, "Mario, I think you are experiencing symbolic confusion in regard to Melanie." Not really understanding what symbolic confusion was, I took this to prayer. The Lord answered my prayer by giving me insight through two troublesome incidents.

The first incident happened at a banquet for the theater company Melanie and I worked for. We were separately invited. Along with other members of the company, we were seated at a long, thin rectangular table, and I sat opposite Melanie. While we were having dinner, my body kept leaning in toward Melanie as if magnetically attracted to her. Suddenly, my tie plopped into my food. Consciously, I resisted the physical urge to get closer to her. Despite my efforts, my body uncontrollably kept leaning over. If this continued, I knew both my shirt and tie would be covered with my dinner. Finally, flustered (and embarrassed) by my feelings and actions, I simply excused myself and moved to another table.

The second incident was a date with a girl I'll call Louise. Because it was clear that Melanie had no intention of dating me, I attempted to get interested in other women. I thought this might help me overcome my feelings for Melanie. I met Louise at church. She was a very mature and intelligent Christian woman—and also very pretty. We began spending time together—getting to know one another.

One night Louise and I went out to dinner. Throughout the evening I was so preoccupied with thoughts of Melanie, I had to think twice before calling Louise by name lest I accidently call her Melanie. During dinner Louise's many feminine qualities reminded me of Melanie—her delicate angora sweater, the string of pearls round her neck, the way her hair curled up right before touching her shoulders, her beautiful smile. Yet in reality Louise looked nothing like Melanie. In fact, they were quite different from each other, with one exception—they were both very feminine. After this evening, I knew I was not ready for a relationship with any woman. So Louise and I met once again for dinner and peaceably ended the romantic phase of our friendship.

After these two incidents, I connected these potent feelings for Melanie to the neurotic feelings I previously had had for a young man while I was still afflicted with homosexuality. Now I knew something was wrong inside me. Leanne's counsel about symbolic confusion came back to me.

In my heart, femininity and Melanie were inextricably linked. Melanie was the standard I used to recognize the feminine in other women and in myself. As a symbol in my heart, Melanie was a shrine to womanhood, a tribute to all that is feminine. When seeing something feminine, I immediately thought of Melanie. While with Louise, I had unconsciously projected onto her my heart's symbol of femininity—Melanie.

I related to Melanie from the immature posture of my need to possess her, to have her. Much like my previous cannibal compulsion toward men, I had a ravenous hunger for Melanie. I wanted to take from Melanie a part of myself I was not in touch with. Melanie symbolized a part of my feminine I was separated from and needed to integrate with.

Like the immature love we saw in *Romeo and Juliet*, my thoughts about Melanie all too quickly turned to marriage. Yet I had failed to ask myself some important and necessary questions, such as, "Does she love me?" Like Romeo, I never really saw the flesh-and-blood person who stood before me. I saw Melanie only as I projected onto her my idealized image of woman. Melanie was my Juliet.

Once this insight sank deep into my heart, I became aware of the sin of trying to find my happiness in the creature rather than in the Creator. Like Romeo with Juliet, I held Melanie in my heart as a shrine. Therefore, I needed to repent of idolatry.

In my neighborhood group that week, I confessed my sin and repented of it. Then members in the group ministered to me with the laying on of hands to receive the forgiveness of sins and healing. After receiving God's forgiveness, I spontaneously broke out into calls of love for Jesus. Because all my religious awe was directed toward Him and no longer confusedly toward woman in unconscious idol worship, I was free to love and worship Jesus all the more.

The real danger Melanie and I were both spared, primarily because Melanie did not respond to me, was marriage. Had I married her, I might have awakened one morning to find she did not live up to my idealized image of woman—the perfect romantic other. This happens to many newlyweds. In most cases it does not mean they have married amiss as much as that they need to love in a more mature way. However in my case, my "love" for Melanie might have easily turned to hatred, as this beautiful face of other-sex ambivalence might suddenly have switched to reveal the ugly face of other-sex ambivalence.

The Feared, Despised Other

In one corner our heart may hold the image of woman as idealized, someone to be worshiped and adored (a holy shrine). In the other corner we may view woman as someone to be feared and despised.

Shortly after I moved to Milwaukee, Leanne Payne graciously offered her friendship and counsel. Though I knew many people would gladly have embraced the opportunity to work with Leanne and to learn from her, I did not. In fact, I felt a strange resistance to getting too close to Leanne, while at the same time I felt genuine love for her.

I had approach-avoidance feelings. Unknowingly, I was experiencing other-sex ambivalence toward Leanne also. But instead of seeing her as my idealized image of the other sex, I saw her as both idealized and devalued. Part of me also viewed Leanne as the feared, despised other.

Initially, I rationalized these ambivalent feelings by thinking negative thoughts about Leanne. Basically I blamed the ambivalence on her, thinking these feelings were somehow her fault.

Actually, I felt sincere love for Leanne and appreciated all she had done for me. Her books filled me with deep gratitude for her caring and understanding heart. Additionally, God had used *The Broken Image* to return me to Himself. For that reason alone I was grateful to her. However, when I was with Leanne, I could never courteously thank her for the way God had used her in my life. I had difficulty looking her in the eye, much less giving her a word of thanks.

On several occasions, Leanne invited me to her home for a meal and for fellowship with other Christians. Together we shared what the Lord was doing in our lives. Never did she show condescension—the mature Christian looking down at me in my immature state. She always honored me as a person and as a fellow Christian. When I shared my struggles, Leanne often offered to pray for me. On many occasions, I called her and asked for prayer. During these prayer times I rarely felt anything happening (sometimes my mind was too busy thinking ambivalent thoughts about Leanne). However, several hours after these prayer times, the power of the Holy Spirit fell upon me, and healing entered in.

One reason I had difficulty receiving from Leanne was that I did not want to be indebted to her. Yet from reading her books and from her friendship, I knew she was one of the few people in Christendom who could really help me. So I forced myself to receive from her, but I resented it.

Later, I read Walter Trobisch's book *All a Man Can Be* and realized why. The book is written in three parts; sufferings unique to men, how man reacts to his sufferings, and how man is redeemed from his sufferings. About the sufferings of the insecure man, he writes:

> The man, the proud conqueror, the monumental figure, has to admit when it comes down to the bare facts that he is dependent upon woman. He has been on the receiving end since the beginning of his life—and it is the woman who is the giver.
>
> All over the world it is the same story. The one who is on the receiving end always feels inferior, put down in the face of the one who gives.[16]

According to Trobisch, this is man's predicament until he brings all these feelings into the redeeming light of Christ and repents. Not only must we men acknowledge our need to receive from woman, but in order to be whole men we must find the humility to ask for her help as need be. Trobisch continues: "A redeemed man is one who is not afraid to ask for directions. In this way he leads. Only those who are led can lead."[17]

Leanne also appeared in my dreams. When I told her about these dreams, she gently reminded me I was not dreaming of her literally. Rather, I was dreaming about that part of myself she symbolized to me. This was difficult for me to grasp at first, so I quietly held it in my heart before the Lord in prayer for understanding.

Toward the end of my first year in Milwaukee, I attended a conference where Leanne was one of the main speakers. During this conference, Leanne met privately with me and lovingly confronted me about the other-sex ambivalence I had toward her. However, because this was still at an unconscious level, I told her I was not aware of any ambivalence.

It is important to emphasize here that because of the unconscious nature of other-sex ambivalence projections, people are often unaware of what they are doing. For this reason, any confrontation must be properly timed and should be done by one who is trusted and respected. Up to this point, Leanne's counsel and prayers had always borne good fruit in my life, so I prayerfully took her words to the Lord. Additionally, I knew she loved me and that what she said could possibly be true.

Returning to my seat, I waited for Leanne to begin the next lecture. Silently, I sat there praying to the Lord Jesus and lifting up Leanne's loving confrontation. Then Leanne approached the podium and began her lecture. As she spoke, she gestured with her hands as usual, but for the first time I noticed that she was wearing red fingernail polish. As I looked at those red nails flying through space with her every gesture, like bits of fire on the end of a stick, I began to feel uneasy. I thought to myself, Leanne sort of looks like a witch up there with those long red fingernails. My mind began to run away with me. Oh, Lord, maybe she is really a witch in disguise. Maybe I've mistakenly gotten myself involved with a cult. Suddenly, I felt both fear of and contempt for Leanne.

Full of anxiety about my thoughts, I focused back in on the lecture. At that moment Leanne said, "Sometimes when I am working with a man who is being healed of gender confusion, all I need to do is to put on red fingernail polish to constellate his othersex ambivalence."

Well, that is exactly what happened to me. Just as the feminine qualities in Melanie called forth in me thoughts and feelings connected with my idealized image of woman, Leanne at this moment called forth the polar extreme of these thoughts and feelings. Her painted fingernails called to consciousness my feared and despised image of woman. The manifestation of this symbolic confusion started first with my general ambivalent thoughts toward Leanne, got stirred up with my discomfort with her red fingernails, and culminated in my projecting onto her my heart's feared, despised image of woman as witchy.

Red fingernails to many men call up images of woman as the seductress, the witch, the one who controls man by manipulating him. Most men are not aware when this is happening. Had Leanne not confronted me moments before her lecture and had I not been asking Jesus to search my heart, I might have left that meeting believing a lie about Leanne and in great deception about the state of my own heart.

As I look back, I realize I treated Leanne emotionally much the way people treated Joan of Arc in her day. One moment I saw Leanne as "the Saint," an obedient woman of God; the next I saw her as "the Witch," burning her at the stake with my ambivalent thoughts.

St. Joan is a sad example of what many women throughout history have experienced. History records a disproportionate number of women being burned as witches in comparison to men being burned as warlocks (or sorcerers). This is not to say that real witches do not exist or even that woman in her brokenness does not have control issues to deal with. However, the Christian response to a real witch is to lead her to the cross, not burn her at the stake.

Even in the church today, it is common for a strongly gifted or a domineering or manipulative woman to be accused of having a spirit of witchcraft. What many fail to understand is that a woman may become domineering and manipulative in relationship with a passive male. For the married woman, this may be her only defense to hold her family together or the only way she knows to motivate her husband to provide for her children. The problem could be just as easily spiritualized by labeling the man as having a spirit of Caspar Milquetoast.

I have heard pastors say of a certain women, "She has a Jezebel spirit," or "she has a spirit of witchcraft." I even received a report of one woman who was pushed up against a wall while a witch-hunting ambivalent male tried to cast out a Jezebel spirit from her. But never have I heard of a controlling and manipulative man being accused of having an Ahab spirit (Jezebel's equally evil husband in the Old Testament) or a spirit of Simon the Sorcerer. I believe that those men in the business of naming Jezebel spirits are suffering from other-sex ambivalence. Under these circumstances they operate not in the gift of discernment of demons, but rather in a fleshly suspicion of demons coupled with other-sex ambivalence.

Ambivalence, whether toward the same sex or the other sex, is related to what psychologists call transference. Transference is the projecting onto someone in the present, relational dynamics from persons we have known in the past. There are positive transferences such as the idealized view of woman in other-sex ambivalence. There are also negative transferences such as the feared, despised view of woman in other-sex ambivalence. In order to be healed, we must face our transferences head-on and receive insight into how they originated. But often we resist this insight. In fact, resistance may manifest at the very time a transference is most obvious. As we saw with the television evangelist, after his problem became public knowledge and he had openly confessed his sin, he refused the help his denomination offered.

Pride fuels resistance and prevents us from openly facing our sins and shortcomings. Then deception often enters in. Dick Keyes writes:

> More often than we care to admit, deception is the way we cope with threatening situations and personal guilt. Dishonesty can come as naturally as the reflex action of blinking the eye or raising the hand to protect the face. [18]

When we deceive ourselves into thinking that problems within our souls do not exist, we usually blame others. Once we find someone to blame, our problem is deflected onto another person. Such is the case with the man afflicted with other-sex ambivalence who refuses to face his problem. He takes literally his heart's symbolic confusion of woman, seeing her as someone to be feared and despised. Projecting this distortion onto a real woman, he deceives himself and others into believing she is a witch or has a Jezebel spirit.

The Women of My Dreams

Figures of speech in literature generally substitute one thing for another. A figure of speech may have either a literal or a figurative meaning. The persons who appear in our dreams may be either literal or figurative representations of a part of ourselves. Once I understood this, I asked God for the interpretation of my dreams.

The dreams I had of Melanie and Leanne actually revealed places in my heart that needed healing. In my childhood home,

I had witnessed woman only in the negative light of degrading submission. It was symptomatic of my broken condition that my heart was searching for the true feminine, for true woman. In my brokenness, my feminine was crying out for expression, trying to find meaning. My heart yearned for images of whole women. This yearning translated into my dreams. Leanne and Melanie represented the true feminine in me.

Leanne, as author, teacher, and minister, symbolized my feminine in its God-given creative giftedness. In her walk with Christ and her expertise as a pastoral caregiver, I saw in Leanne the Christian maturity the Lord was leading me into. The more contact I had with her, the more she called forth in me both the healed and the unhealed dimensions of my feminine. Melanie represented my feminine as it ought to have been—alive, free to respond to God, and joyful. Just as I came into the awareness of the otherliness of woman, I met Melanie. She also represented real woman—the right partner for real man. In her presence I often felt as if all the healthy masculinity within me was bursting forth like a young buck dancing in a meadow. Just as Romeo afflicted with star-crossed love saw his soul in Juliet, so too did I see my soul in Melanie.

When we do not receive healing for other-sex ambivalence and the symbolic confusion of our hearts, we are often bound by the sin of envy. In my brokenness, I envied Leanne's gifts as a writer and a minister. I also envied Melanie for having a freedom of spirit I thought unavailable to men. Had I not repented of this sin, I would never have come to love woman aright, never come to appreciate her giftedness, and never come to own for myself some of the goodness in Melanie and Leanne I previously envied. Without healing, I would have forever projected my feminine onto woman, been unable to have healthy relationships with women, and remained alienated from much of my own soul.

When Man Projects His Soul onto Woman

Soul (a word used sparingly in modern translations of the Bible) is not a part of human nature but characterizes it in its totality. The word soul in both Hebrew *(nepheth)* and Greek *(psuche)* is in the feminine gender. The soul in every person is feminine; it is one's soul that responds (the feminine) to God's initiative (the masculine). About our feminine relationship to our masculine God, Dr. Donald Bloesch writes:

> God is not a man, but, for the most part, he chooses to relate him-self to us as masculine. Yahweh, unlike the gods and goddesses of the pagan religions, has no consort. We, the church, are his consort, and this means that the church constitutes the feminine dimension of the sacred. Israel is portrayed in the Old Testament as the wife of Yahweh (Isaiah 54:5; Hosea 2:2, 7, 16) and the Daughter of Zion (Isaiah 16:1; 62:11; Jeremiah 6:2, 23; Lamenta-tions 1:6; 2:18). The church is depicted as the bride of Christ in the New Testament.[19]

Kevin, whose story introduced this chapter, and I had one thing in common—we were alienated from woman and from the fem-inine within ourselves. As a result, we were alienated from aspects of our very souls. You will recall that Romeo referred to Juliet as "my soul." About the feminine nature of the soul, Ruth Tiffany Barnhouse writes:

> It is no accident that in the dreams of individuals as well as in myths (which are the dreams of the race), feminine figures are always chosen to represent the soul. Today's feminist writers are often outraged, and male theologians often embarrassed, by some of the medieval debates on the question of whether or not women had souls. What is forgotten is that one of the most important arguments was the reason women cannot be said to have a soul is because they are soul.[20]

Karl Stern in his book *The Flight from Woman* chronicles the historical flight of men from the feminine. As a result, we men have not only lost touch with the good of feminine qualities as they exist in all humanity, but we have lost touch with our very souls. Within the context of Christian marriage, I often hear men say, "My wife is the one who hears from God in prayer; I get all my direction from the Word" (meaning through rational analysis of the Bible, which is necessary to a healthy Christian walk, but should not be the only way we relate to God). These men invariably believe women are primarily intuitive and men are primarily rational. Though feminine wisdom includes intuitive aspects, just as masculine wisdom includes rational aspects, it is wrong to relinquish possession of one of these forms of wisdom because of our gender.

Women in these marriages often agree with their husbands and thus abdicate their minds, simply "submitting" to his thinking. They are not exercising the masculine analytical part of their minds, and the men are not exercising the feminine intuitive part of theirs. Leanne Payne writes:

> We cannot lose the feminine principle without weakening and eventually losing the masculine; we cannot retain the good of the masculine discursive reason apart from the feminine intuitive mind and heart. All the precious and colorful strands of reality are wonderfully interconnected. To discard one strand is to loosen and thereby endanger the whole framework of life.[21]

When men alienated from the feminine come to me for help, they often recount with great remorse that their prayer life is uninviting. In touch only with masculine reasoning, such a man's prayers may be nothing more than a series of dry rational statements about God. In prayer he does most of the talking and rarely waits in response (the feminine) to receive from God that word He is sending. Separated from the feminine qualities dormant within himself, he will project his feminine onto his wife and expect her to carry a part of their relationship with God that he should be experiencing also. If a man is not rightly related to woman, he will not be rightly related to his own soul (the feminine within himself). Distorted views of woman in his heart may also parallel a problem in his ability to relate to God.

When man's other-sex ambivalence is confronted and brought into the light of God's truth through prayer, the symbolic confusion underneath disengages. The memories of the sin of woman against him or his sins against her will come flooding to his conscious mind. The pain of never being rightly related to mother, of not having a sense of being in her love will come to the surface. In prayer before the cross of Jesus, a man can forgive the offenses of the past, receive forgiveness for his sins against woman, and receive healing of effects of a childhood where mother was never really there for him. He can also confess his offenses against woman. In this way, a man comes free from polarized views of woman lodged in his deep heart. The most extreme polarity is the classic virgin/whore complex, but other-sex ambivalence has many gradations. Simply realizing that his hope for the perfect idealized woman will never be fulfilled or his image of the feared despised woman will never prove to be a reality is often enough to begin healing in a man.

Once I came to see Leanne and Melanie aright and ceased to project onto them the unhealed dimensions of my feminine, something remarkable resulted. I had a greatly increased sense of being. If it is in the love of the feminine (mother) that we come into a secure sense of being; then it follows that when we relate aright to the feminine both in ourselves and in others, our own sense of being deepens. Rather than projecting parts of myself onto women, I integrated with "my lady soul," and she found a home within me.

Integrating with the Feminine

With my healing from other-sex ambivalence clearly underway, I found myself becoming more outwardly directed toward women. For the first time in my life I wanted to give to woman, to bless her. The man in the throes of other-sex ambivalence cannot give to woman. He sees her as either unapproachable and beyond his reach, or as someone to be feared, whom he must control lest she get out of hand, or as someone to be avoided altogether.

No longer bound to the old distorted images my heart held of woman, I was now free to feel all the repressed emotions I had toward women. Though most of these feelings were good, some were not. In disengaging my heart's symbolic confusion of woman, all the illogical attitudes, emotions, and behaviors arising from these broken images of woman came flooding to consciousness.

In my relationship to my mother, I was now free to allow all my negative feelings for her, which I had suppressed since childhood, to surface. However, by this time I knew better than to annihilate her with my feelings or to project them onto her and blame her. Instead I applied the cross of Jesus to those memories by forgiving her or asking forgiveness for myself as need be.

I now came face to face with the reality that in the adverse conditions at home, caused primarily by my father's behaviors, my mother could not give to us children emotionally because she was emotionally spent. I also saw that I had bonded to her in a negative way in an attempt to protect her from my father. Many times she had confided in me about certain things that were not appropriate for a mother to share with her son. I needed to establish the proper boundaries for an adult son to have with his mother.

In order to become healthy, I needed to separate my identity from hers. This would have occurred naturally had my father affirmed me as a man, thus coming between her and me. But he did not do this. Additionally, I was used to being there for my mother at all times—in a way a husband ought to be for his wife. Finally, I had to relinquish my need to protect her and entrust her care to Jesus. This was painful for my mother. She felt I had deserted her. But this step was necessary for my emotional well-being and maturation into manhood.

Before the Lord I dealt with my feelings about my mother, both negative and positive. As I prayed with trusted friends such as Leanne and those in my neighborhood prayer group, a deeper love for my mother welled up from within me. I began to see the many ways she had genuinely given to me when I was a child. Now sincerely thankful to her, I was free to give her unconditional love.

In the years that followed I dated several women. These were healthy relationships built on respect, mutual interests, and love for Jesus. After several months in one of these relationships, my friend told me, "Mario, sometimes when we are talking, it's as if you put up a wall, and there's no genuine communication between us." Having sensed this invisible wall too, I knew there was still something unresolved in my heart toward women. A few years later, the Lord showed me what this wall was. A deeply repressed fear of abandonment by woman prevented me from trusting her at the deepest levels of my being. For that reason, I could never open my heart fully to commit to a woman in marriage.

This fear that a woman would abandon me was rooted in my separation from my mother when I was hospitalized for over a month during infancy. I developed infantile separation anxiety, which resulted in genital tension manifesting later in life as a dread-ridden masturbation. Also an unconscious sense of abandonment ensued.

Once again the Lord used my relationship with Leanne Payne as the context within which He would constellate and heal this problem in relating with woman. Just as six years earlier my other-sex ambivalence had manifested as a projection onto Leanne, so too did this long-repressed infantile fear of abandonment.

By this time I had known Leanne for nearly eight years. Over these years our relationship became one of trusted friendship. Originally, I had contacted Leanne as a pastoral caregiver for help. Thereafter our relationship grew into casual friendship. Over time our friendship deepened, and Leanne became a spiritual mother to me. Additionally, God had called me to work closely with her at Pastoral Care Ministries, and she regarded me as a trusted colleague.

This trust built between us over those eight years was very therapeutic. Through our relationship, the Lord rebuilt in me a previously broken structure of trust. Such structures of trust are normally built in early infancy. However, due to my mother's emotionally deprived state and the trauma of my father's constant abuse, along with my own separation anxiety, the normal trust never developed between us. In fact, Leanne was the first woman I completely trusted. My ability to trust an older, wiser woman such as Leanne enabled me to begin trusting other women.

In the terminology of classical psychoanalysis, my relationship with Leanne included a strong element of transference. Transference is a common human psychological process by which people in the present day are substituted for people we related to in the past. Transferences happen all the time in the context of friendships, work relationships, Christian fellowship, and marriages. Transferences often happen within the context of the church, which is uniquely equipped to minister healing to the emotionally wounded. When healthy, the church becomes a new family in which we can grow into maturity. Paul writing to Timothy says, "Do not rebuke an older man but exhort him as you would a father; treat younger men like brothers, older women like mothers, younger women like sisters, in all purity" (1 Timothy 5:1 RSV).

Some transferences are stronger than others, depending on the emotional woundedness of the one doing the transferring. In my case, the emotional woundedness caused me to unconsciously turn Leanne into a mother substitute.

There are both positive and negative transferences. Initially, transferences are almost always positive. Genuine positive attributes in a healthy person enable positive transferences to develop between such a person and an emotionally wounded one. Initially, I viewed Leanne positively as exceedingly loving, gracious, kind, full of faith, and generous. Indeed, these are real virtues in Leanne's character. Positive transferences enable an emotionally wounded person to trust others. For that reason, many therapists work to model unconditional positive regard—empathy and respect toward their clients to create an environment where positive transferences may occur. Such transferences can slip into idealizations of the one being transferred upon. This too occurred early in my relationship with Leanne, and the idealization was properly dealt with.

Positive transferences nearly always progress into negative transferences. This is part of the process of healing. Initially, this occurred as I projected onto Leanne my heart's confused image of woman as controlling and witchy. And as I worked through this confusion, my relationships with all women improved. It was years later that my repressed fear of abandonment by woman surfaced. This could only happen in the context of a trusting relationship (a positive transference). The more I trusted Leanne, the more vulnerable I was in sharing my past hurts with her, and the more this repressed abandonment was likely to surface.

My negative transferences regarding abandonment occurred during several healing missions over the period of a year. The ministry was growing very rapidly, and with growth came conflict. In the context of these conflicts, Leanne and I had several disagreements. Rather than objectively naming where I disagreed, I had hostile reactions to Leanne (hostility is common in negative transferences). At first I suppressed my hostile reactions and disagreements out of fear of abandonment. I thought that if she knew I disagreed, then she would cease to be my friend. In my childhood home, every time I had disagreed with my father, the rest of the family, including my mother, had abandoned me and come to his defense.

One time after a healing mission, my repressed hostility erupted as Leanne and I discussed one of these disagreements. To my surprise, I projected such rage onto Leanne that I seriously wounded her. At that point Leanne told me I was in the midst of a transference. But I could not fully receive this.

When transferences take a negative turn, resistance (a psychological concept) will also surface. Resistance serves at least three neurotic purposes. First, it serves to deny that the transference has turned negative. My initial suppression of hostil-ity was itself an attempt to deny the negative transference. Additionally, my inability to fully see the negative transference once it surfaced in projected rage was also part of this denial. Second, resistance serves as a defense against uncovering repressed issues. Resistance in me served to repress a major unresolved issue of abandonment and related rage. Third, resistance serves to scapegoat the person being transferred upon. At first I thought some of my hostile reactions toward Leanne were legitimate.

Again I turn to Dr. Gerard van den Aardweg's comment on resistance:

> We can understand what Freud meant when he discussed the phenomenon of resistance he observed in the treatment of many neurotics and which made on him "the deepest impression of all," giving him "the feeling that there is a force at work that defends itself with all possible means against cure and that obstinately clings to illness and sufferings."[22]

Overcoming resistance is central to psychological healing. Without pressing through resistance, the person seeking psychological healing simply remains stuck in a hostile state of negative transference.

After I returned home from this mission, the issues underlying this negative transference began to surface. In attempting to resolve the wounding I had caused Leanne by my rage, Leanne and I had several phone conversations and exchanged letters. In one of Leanne's letters, she expressed the hurt she was feeling and said that the trust between us was now broken. I took her statement to mean that our friendship was now over. This misperception was itself a projection. I misinterpreted the letter to mean that Leanne had abandoned me. Because she had been a spiritual mother to me and I had unconsciously substituted her for my real mother, I felt I was losing a mother figure. This constellated the loss I had experienced as an infant when I was hospitalized and separated from my mother.

Repressed memories of that time began to surface. An infant in a prolonged state of separation from its mother perceives her absence as a loss akin to death. Not only does the child feel abandoned and suffer separation anxiety, but it also experiences deep grief. Memories of prolonged separation from mother sometimes surface as repressed feelings rather than remembered images of the past. The perceived loss of Leanne's friendship elicited from me these repressed feelings of abandonment and intense grief.

When these powerful feelings came up, I did not know what they were. Initially I was stricken with anxiety. My heart beat so rapidly I could see my chest move up and down when I was lying down. I slept only a few hours each night. Filled with infantile fear, I developed a strong startle reaction. The smallest noise caused me to jump as if a bomb had gone off behind me. A profound loneliness and internal emptiness were my only companions.

Not since I had come out of denial regarding my father's evil behaviors had I been in such intense pain. The only difference now was that this was an unrelenting pain. It never ceased, not for one moment day or night. I did not think it was possible for a human being to bear such continuous mental and emotional pain. While I had faced emotional suffering before, I did not know if my sanity could survive this time.

In the midst of the pain, the Lord reminded me of Elizabeth Goudge's book, *The Scent of Water*. It is the story of a woman named Mary who suffers from a black depression that she tries to hide from the world. One day an Anglican vicar comes to visit her. Questioning Mary about her depression, he asks, "You're afraid of it?"

She replies, "Of course I am. I'm terrified."

"Why?" he asked. "If you lose your reason, you lose it into the hands of God."[23]

This was Mary's secret fear, the fear of losing her mind. She dare not speak of it lest she bring it into being.

It was Jung who said that "neurosis is always a substitute for legitimate suffering." Over the previous eight years my homosexual defenses of same-sex ambivalence, other-sex ambivalence, and related symbolic confusion had been disengaged. The homosexual neurosis was no longer intact enough to resort to in lieu of legitimate suffering. I simply had to suffer and face my deepest, most secret fear. Such fears are what some psychoanalysts call a pathogenic secret. Occasionally it would rear its head and then submerge again into a sea of defenses.

Like Mary in *The Scent of Water*, my pathogenic secret was the fear of losing my mind. The Anglican vicar eventually says to Mary, "My dear, Love—your God—is a trinity. There are three necessary prayers, and they have three words each. They are these, 'Lord have mercy.' 'Thee I adore.' 'Into Thy hands.' Not difficult to remember. If in times of distress you hold to these, you will do well."[24]

After two weeks of unending anxiety and little sleep, I faced this pathogenic secret fear of losing my mind in the pain of abandonment. Lying on my bed, with my head dangling over the edge of my mattress, I prayed to Jesus, "This is it, Lord. I'm about to lose my mind. It feels as if my head is about to fall off my body. I'm trusting You are here to catch it." Then remembering the vicar's prayer, I prayed, "Lord, have mercy. Thee I adore. Into Thy hands." As I repeatedly prayed this little prayer, the fear of losing my mind began to leave. Then the Lord spoke to my heart and told me to call Phil, one of my prayer partners.

That evening Phil and I met for prayer. I was reminded of a scar on my right ankle left by the surgical intravenous implant through which I was fed during my month-long hospitalization as an infant. We invoked the name of Jesus and entered into His presence. Then Phil anointed the scar on my right ankle with holy oil. Immediately, a memory came up. It was of a metal pole with a hook curved upward at the top end. My right foot was suspended from the hook, and I could see the intravenous feeding line going into my ankle. A strap across my pelvis held me down so I could not move. I was all alone. This was the actual memory of abandonment in the hospital.

As the prayer continued, Phil saw a thick underground root system coiled around my spine. I too saw this coiling root and named it as the fear of abandonment. As Phil prayed to release me from it, my whole spine began to move in a most unusual way. I felt a demonic presence leave me. Gradually this root of abandonment began to uncoil and leave me. This took some time. Once the root was gone, Phil saw the Lord Jesus remove tiny hair-like follicles that were part of the root, and then Jesus filled every empty crevice with His love. Next I forgave the medical authorities for not allowing my mother to visit me during my stay in the hospital. Also I asked the Lord to forgive my sins against Leanne. Finally, I realized that the rage I had projected onto her was repressed infantile rage at being abandoned.

That night, for the first time in two weeks, I slept for eight hours uninterruptedly. When I awakened the next morning, I knew I had turned a corner in my healing. For the first time in weeks I had the soundness of mind to have a morning devotion. My Bible reading for that day included:

> Set your minds on things above, not on earthly things. For you died, and your life is now hidden with Christ in God. . . . But now you must rid yourselves of all such things as these: anger, rage, malice, slander, and filthy language from your lips. Do not lie to each other, since you have taken off your old self with its practices and have put on the new self, which is being renewed in knowl-

edge in the image of its Creator. . . . Therefore, as God's chosen people, holy and dearly loved, clothe yourselves with compassion, kindness, humility, gentleness and patience. Bear with each other and forgive whatever grievances you may have against one another. Forgive as the Lord forgave you. And over all these virtues put on love, which binds them all together in perfect unity. (Colossians 3:2–3, 8–10, 12–14)

Putting on God's love and humility, I wrote to Leanne and asked her forgiveness for the way I had projected abandonment rage onto her. In asking for her forgiveness, I broke through the resistance that had kept the negative transference in place. She graciously forgave me.

In the year that followed, I entered into therapy to better understand the dynamics of these transferences. I came to see that my positive transference onto Leanne laid the foundation of trust that allowed the infantile memories of abandonment to fully surface in the context of a negative transference. Leanne remains a dear friend, colleague, teacher, and spiritual mother to me. But now my relationship to her is hallmarked by more maturity and is free of negative transferences.

Six years earlier, my initial release from other-sex ambivalence had changed all my relationships with women for the better. This had enabled me to begin loving women aright. Gradually, the Lord revealed that there were layers to my confusion toward woman. At the right time, He brought me back to a place of suffering and abandonment to heal me more deeply. This freed me all the more to love woman in the right way.

Freedom from this confusion of other-sex ambivalence came to me in at least four ways. First, I practiced the presence of God and allowed Him to search my heart for any distorted images of the other sex. More than anything, I needed patience and grace to process all that was coming up from within my heart. As obvious distorted images, feelings, and thoughts about women came up, I prayed to God to take these distortions and replace them with good and real images of the other sex. Sometimes I had to simply wait in His presence for a long time—days, weeks, months before this happened.

Second, I came into right relationship with women in the context of the Body of Christ. Remember Martin Buber's words, "All real living is meeting." Unless we are willing to encounter (meet) people and work through our relational difficulties, we will never be healed enough to truly love. Christian fellowship played a most significant part in resymbolizing my heart's image of woman. In the church I witnessed healthy men and women relating rightly to each other. But I also learned to recognize when they related amiss. At first I had difficulty recognizing normal behavior between the sexes because I did not know what normal was. When I had a question, I asked a trusted Christian friend.

Third, at times I went directly to women and asked their forgiveness for ways I had hurt them. Five years ago one life-changing reconciliation occurred between myself and a woman named Allison. We had become friends while working together at a French restaurant in Milwaukee in the summer of 1980. Shortly after I moved to Boston in autumn of 1981, Allison also moved to Boston. In Boston we shared a lovely apartment and lived together for about a year. During this time we discovered that our interests were very similar. Our relationship took on the overtones of a marriage, with one exception—we were never intimate physically. It was painful for both Allison and myself when we realized that the only thing preventing a romantic relationship was my homosexuality. We had played with the fires of male/female relating, and instead of our souls being warmed through reciprocal giving, we were burned to the heart. Once I realized what had happened in our relationship, I hastily found another apartment and moved out.

After some healing from homosexuality, the Lord showed me how I had sinned against Allison. I had taken from her the normal love a woman gives to a man, but had not given back any real love. Additionally, I unknowingly had exposed her to dangers on occasions when I brought home one-night stands from gay bars. And in moving out of our apartment so quickly, I conveyed rejection.

Now, years later, I was returning home from a healing mission and had a four-hour layover in San Francisco. Just as the plane landed, the Lord spoke to my heart and said, "Call Allison." I had forgotten that Allison had moved to San Francisco. After looking up her number in the phone book, I called her and asked if we could meet. She agreed to come to the airport providing her car didn't break down. Once she arrived, she told me that earlier in the evening she had tried going out, but had car trouble and had to return home. Surprisingly, her car worked perfectly all the way to the airport. (It seemed the Lord had arranged our meeting.) While sharing with her how the Lord had healed me of homosexuality, I told her how heavy my heart felt whenever I thought back on our days together in Boston. Then I confessed my sins against her and asked her forgiveness.

"Mario, every time we met after you moved out on me, I sensed a cloud of guilt around you. Of course I forgive you," she responded.

"Good. Now I can die in peace."

Fourth, as my relating toward women continued to mature, I learned to walk out "instant" love relationships with women. The words of Song of Songs 2:7 have become my motto for romantic relationships: "Do not arouse or awaken love until it so desires." For my own good, I've promised myself not to consider marriage with any woman until I've had a healthy friendship with her for at least a year.

When as a teenager I first met Jesus personally, the church offered me no healing for my homosexuality. Consequently, I feared that what I believed about the gospel of Jesus was untrue. Even though I strayed from the faith and entered into the gay lifestyle, Jesus remained faithful to me. He sought me out. He led me out of homosexuality and into the hands of loving Christians who knew how to minister healing into my sexuality. He promised me that I would help Him deliver homosexual people from the bondage of their sin. Over the last ten years He has used me to minister healing to thousands of people overcoming sexual brokenness. Today I know that everything I ever believed about the goodness of God and the faithfulness of Jesus has proved true.

Jesus said, "A new command I give you: Love one another. As I have loved you, so you must love one another" (John 13:34). In my trek out of homosexuality and into heterosexuality, God has been teaching me how to love aright. The goal of the Christian life is to become like Jesus and to love as He loved. Jesus works His life into us by setting love in order.

To God alone be the glory.

Notes

Chapter 1: "Choose!"

1. William Barclay, *The Gospel of Matthew*, Vol. 1 (Philadelphia: Westminster Press, 1956), p. 44.

Chapter 2: *Coming Out of Denial*

1. Hemfelt, Minirth, Meier, *Love Is a Choice* (Nashville: Thomas Nelson Publishers, 1989), p. 57.

2. Dick Keyes, *Beyond Identity* (Ann Arbor, Mich.: Servant Books, 1984), p. 69.

3. Conrad Baars and Anna Terruwe, *Healing the Unaffirmed: Recognizing Deprivation Neurosis* (New York: Alba House, a division of Society of St. Paul, 1972), p. 36.

4. Ibid., p. 13.

5. Diagnostic and Statistical Manual of Mental Disorders, 3d rev. ed. (Washington, DC: American Psychiatric Assn., 1987), p. 247.

6. Scott Peck, *People of the Lie* (New York: Simon and Schuster, 1985), p. 9.

7. Kenelm Footer, and Mary John Ronayne, *I Catherine—Selected Writings of Catherine of Siena* (London: St. James Place, 1980), p. 43.

8. Leanne Payne, *Crisis in Masculinity* (Wheaton: Crossway Books, 1985), pp. 65–66.

9. Corrie ten Boom, *The Hiding Place* (Minneapolis: World Wide Pictures, 1971), p. 215.

10. Gary R. Sweeten, *Breaking Free from the Past* (Cincinnati: Christian Information Committee, 1980).

11. Gerard van den Aardweg, *Homosexuality and Hope* (Ann Arbor, Mich.: Servant Books, 1985), p. 62.

12. St. Augustine, *On Christian Doctrine*, trans. D.W. Robertson, Jr. (New York: Bobbs-Merrill Publishers, 1958, 1976), p. 54.

Chapter 3: Disordered Love

1. Leanne Payne, *Crisis in Masculinity* (Wheaton: Crossway Books, 1985), p. 19.

2. Ruth Tiffany Barnhouse, *Homosexuality: A Symbolic Confusion* (New York: Seabury Press, 1977), p. 76.

3. Leanne Payne, *The Healing Presence* (Wheaton: Crossway Books, 1989), p. 131.

4. Ray S. Anderson, *On Being Human* (Grand Rapids: William B. Eerdmans Publishing, 1982), p. 110.

5. C. S. Lewis, *Perelandra* (New York: Macmillan Publishing, 1965), p. 200.

6. Donald Bloesch, *The Battle for the Trinity* (Ann Arbor, Mich.: Servant Publications, 1985), pp. 32–33.

7. Donald Bloesch, *Is the Bible Sexist?* (Wheaton: Crossway Books, 1982), p. 66.

8. Paul Ricoeur as quoted by Bloesch, *The Battle for the Trinity*, p. 37.

9. Ibid., p. 39.

10. C. S. Lewis, *That Hideous Strength* (New York: Collier Books, 1962), p. 316.

11. Andrew Comiskey, *Pursuing Sexual Wholeness* (St. Mary, Fla.: Creation House, 1989), p. 115.

12. Payne, *Crisis in Masculinity*, p. 99.

13. Leon Morris, *Testaments of Love* (Grand Rapids: William B. Eerdmans Publishing, 1981), pp. 114–15.

14. Karl Stern, *The Flight from Woman* (New York: Paragon House, 1985), p. 32.

15. Payne, *Crisis in Masculinity*, p. 89.

16. Karen L. Freiberg, *Human Development: A Life-Span Approach*, 2nd ed. (Monterey, Calif.: Wadsworth Health Sciences, 1983), p. 205.

17. Morris, *Testaments of Love*, p. 118.

18. Ibid., p. 120.

19. C. S. Lewis, *The Four Loves* (New York: Harcourt Brace Jovanovich, 1960), p. 135.

20. This understanding of the use of *connaitre* (and *savoir* in the following paragraph) I have gleaned from Karl Stern's book *The Flight from Woman*.

21. Payne, *The Healing Presence*, p. 132.

Chapter 4: Setting Love in Order

1. Margery Williams, *The Velveteen Rabbit* (Garden City, N.Y.: Doubleday, n.d.), p. 17.

2. Leanne Payne, *Crisis in Masculinity* (Wheaton: Crossway Books, 1985), p. 19.

3. Leanne Payne, *The Broken Image* (Wheaton: Crossway Books, 1981), pp. 46–47.

4. Ruth Tiffany Barnhouse, *Homosexuality: A Symbolic Confusion* (New York: Seabury Press, 1977), p. 52.

5. Quoted in Jonathan Bloom-Feshbach et al., *The Psychology of Separation and Loss* (San Francisco: Jossey-Bass Publishers, 1987), p. 91.

6. Ibid., p. 112.

7. David Benner, "The Incarnation as a Metaphor for Psychotherapy," *The Journal of Psychology and Theology* 11, no. 4 (1983): 287–94.

8. Payne, *Broken Image*, p. 59.

9. Josh Bancroft, *Human Sexuality and Its Problems*, 2nd ed. (New York: Churchill Livingstone, 1989), p. 129.

10. Melodie Beattie, *Codependent No More* (New York: Harper and Row, 1987), pp. 56–57.

11. Frank Lake, *Clinical Theology*, abridged by Martin H. Yeomans (New York: Crossroad Publishing, 1987), p. 4.

12. David Shorewood, "A Discarded Son," *New York Times Magazine*, February 9, 1986.

Chapter 5: Christ in Us

1. Father Kallistos Ware, *The Orthodox Way* (Crestwood, N.Y.: St. Vladimir's Orthodox Theological Seminary, 1979), p. 28.

2. Donald Bloesch, *The Struggle of Prayer* (Colorado Springs: Helmers and Howard, Publishers, 1988), p. 36.

3. Justo L. Gonzalez, *The Story of Christianity* (San Francisco: Harper & Row, 1984), p. 84.

4. William Bauer, *A Greek-English Lexicon of the New Testament* (Chicago: University of Chicago Press, 1979), p. 809.

5. Will Herbery, ed., *The Writings of Martin Buber* (New York: Meridian Books, 1956), p. 46.

6. Cyril C. Richardson, "Irenaeus Against Heresies," *Early Christian Fathers* (Philadelphia: Westminster Press, 1970), p. 386.

7. Ibid., p. 377.

8. Athanasius, *The Incarnation of the Word of God* (New York: Macmillan, 1947), p. 46.

9. Oswald Chambers, *My Utmost for His Highest* (New York: Dodd, Mead and Company, 1935, renewed 1963), p. 322.

10. Henri Nouwen, *Behold the Beauty of the Lord* (Notre Dame, Ind.: Ave Maria Press, 1987), p. 22.

11. Emil Brunner, *The Word and the World* (New York: Charles Scribner's Sons, 1931), p. 73.

12. Donald Bloesch, *The Struggle of Prayer*, p. 6.

13. Bernhard W. Anderson, *Out of the Depths* (Philadelphia: Westminster Press, 1983), p. 107.

14. Brunner, *Word and World*, p. 72.

15. Chambers, *My Utmost*, p. 115.

Chapter 6: Loving the Same Sex

1. Kenneth Barker, ed., The NIV Study Bible (Grand Rapids: Zondervan, 1985), textnote, p. 403.

2. J. P. Chaplin, ed., *The Dictionary of Psychology*, 2d rev. ed. (New York: Dell Publishing, 1985), p. 22.

3. William G. Niederland, *The Schreber Case: Psychoanalytic Profile of a Paranoid Personality* (New York: Quadrangle/The New York Times Book Co., 1974), p. 25.

4. Frank Lake, *Clinical Theology* (London: Darton, Longman and Todd, 1966), p. 988.

5. Gerard van den Aardweg, *On the Origins and Treatment of Homosexuality: A Psychoanalytical Reinterpretation* (New York: Praeger Publishers, CBS Ed. and Professional Publications, 1986), p. 32.

6. John Bancroft, *Human Sexuality and Its Problems*, 2nd ed. (New York: Churchill Livingstone, 1989), p. 130.

7. Andrew Comiskey, *The Guidebook to Pursuing Sexual Wholeness* (St. Mary, Fla.: Creation House, 1988), pp. 59–60.

8. Ruth Tiffany Barnhouse, *Homosexuality: A Symbolic Confusion* (New York: Seabury Press, 1977), p. 52.

9. George C. Papademetriou, "Exorcism and the Greek Orthodox Church," in *Exorcism Through the Ages*, ed. St. Elmo Nauman Jr. (New York: Philosophical Library, 1974), pp. 49–50.

10. Ibid., p. 52.

11. Ibid., p. 53.

12. Ibid., p. 50.

Chapter 7: The Hatred of Woman

1. Leanne Payne, *Real Presence* (Wheaton: Crossway Books, 1979), pp. 83–84 (italics hers).

2. Margaret J. Rinck, *Christian Men Who Hate Women* (Grand Rapids: Zondervan, 1990), p. 103.

3. Donald Bloesch, *Is the Bible Sexist?* (Wheaton: Crossway Books, 1982), p. 32.

4. Richard Lovelace, *Homosexuality and the Church* (Tarrytown, N.Y.: Fleming H. Revell, 1978), p. 93.

5. J. B. Skemp, *The Greeks and the Gospels* (Great Britain: Fletcher and Son, 1964), p. 37.

6. Sarah B. Pomeroy, *Goddesses, Whores, Wives and Slaves* (New York: Schocken Books, 1975), p. 219.

7. Dennis Prager, *Ultimate Issues*, April-June 1990, p. 3.

8. Bloesch, *Is the Bible Sexist?*, p. 32.

Chapter 8: Loving the Other Sex

1. Hemfelt, Minirth, Meier, *Love Is a Choice* (Nashville: Thomas Nelson Publishers, 1989), p. 11.

2. Janet G. Woititz, *Struggle for Intimacy* (Pompano Beach, Fla.: Health Communications, 1985), pp. 27–28.

3. Walter Trobisch, *I Married You* (New York: Harper and Row, 1971), p. 13.

4. Leanne Payne, *The Broken Image* (Wheaton: Crossway Books, 1981), pp. 105–6.

5. Karl Stern, *The Flight from Woman* (New York: Paragon House, 1985), p. 19.

6. Trobisch, *I Married You*, p. 73.

7. Stern, *Flight from Woman*, p. 10.

8. William Shakespeare, *The Complete Works of Shakespeare: Tragedies, Comedies, and Sonnets*, vol. 5, ed. Clark and Wright (Philadelphia: Rittenhouse Press [George Barrie and Son], 1899–1915), p. 81.

9. Ibid., pp. 102–3.

10. Ibid., p. 104.

11. Ibid., p. 106.

12. Ibid., p. 111.

13. Ibid., p. 113.

14. Ibid., p. 123.

15. Ibid., p. 172.

16. Walter Trobisch, *All a Man Can Be* (Downers Grove, Ill.: InterVarsity Press, 1983), p. 18.

17. Ibid., p. 64.

18. Dick Keyes, *Beyond Identity* (Ann Arbor, MI: Servant Books, 1984), p. 46.

19. Donald Bloesch, *The Battle for the Trinity* (Ann Arbor, Mich.: Servant Publications, Vine Books, 1985), p. 33.

20. Ruth Tiffany Barnhouse, *Homosexuality: A Symbolic Confusion* (New York: Seabury Press, 1977), p. 87 (italics mine).

21. Leanne Payne, *Crisis in Masculinity* (Wheaton: Crossway Books, 1985), p. 108.

22. Gerard van den Aardweg, *On the Origins and Treatment of Homosexuality: A Psychoanalytical Reinterpretation* (New York: Praeger Publishers, CBS Ed. and Professional Publications), p. 32.

23. Elizabeth Goudge, *The Scent of Water* (New York: Coward-McCann, 1963), p. 113.

24. Ibid., p. 115.